MOUNTAIN BIKE CAPITAL USA™

THE DEVELOPMENT OF A MOUNTAIN BIKE TOWN

SCOTT MICHAEL HICKS II

Abstract

Mountain Bike Capital USA ™

Grand County, Colorado boasts itself as Mountain Bike Capital USA™. Though determining whether or not the county is worthy of such a title would be a worthwhile effort, this book instead focuses on how mountain biking became an economic driver for the mountain towns in Grand County. Through dissecting national trends, local business practices and personal interviews it was clear several groups had a hand in creating this mountain bike reinforced summer economy. The national trends in technology, sales market, and popularity of biking created an opportunity for mountain bike based economies to exist. Grand County proved to be a quality venue for mountain biking, as it already had trails, logging roads, and a service industry ready to host thousands of tourists. The United States Forest Service and local interest groups helped facilitate trail systems in the county, which has grown considerably in the past decades. As mountain biking's popularity rose, signs of cultural change were apparent around the county. Locals, governments, and businesses began to embrace mountain biking as a considerable aspect of the summer tourism industry. Large businesses in the county have taken to mountain biking in new ways, controlling the terrain and morphing the sport into an idealistic experience. Uncovering these elements of the Grand County mountain biking scene created a clearer image of how mountain biking became an economic driver.

In memory of my mother, Beth McLachlan, who always allowed me to work as hard as I wanted and pushed me when it was necessary.

Acknowledgements

A special amount of gratitude to my wife, Courtney Lincoln, for being my sounding board and helping me in every way imaginable during the research and writing process. Without your assistance and support, this project would not be complete. You kept my effort honest and inspired me to continue through the toughest days. Thank you.

Many thanks to the History Department at Adams State University, specifically Dr. Edward Crowther and Dr. Rich Loosbrock for working with me through this project.

Meara McQuain and Keith Sanders were willing to take me in on their day off and give me crucial insight of the Headwaters Trail Alliance operations. Miles Miller, from the United States Forest Service sat down with me for hours, answered emails and presented a new side of mountain biking. Brian Blumenfeld for his detailed editing and valuable suggestions. Thanks to my sister, Taylor McLachlan, for helping with the cover design and direction. Finally, local enthusiasts Maggie Keller, John Cavanaugh, Andy Straus, Kery Harrelson and Jeff McCoy enlightening me as to why people move and live in Grand County.

Contents

Abstract   v

Acknowledgements   xi

1. Mountain Biking and the Context of the West   1

2. Technological Advancements and Popularity   13

3. Grand County as a Recreational Space   33

4. Smokey The Trail Managing Bear   51

5. Promoting Trails and Connecting Islands   69

6. Signs of Cultural Shift   85

7. Ranches, Resorts, and Corporate Mountain Biking   101

8. Mountain Bike Capital USA™?   115

Notes   121

Bibliography   139

1

Mountain Biking and the
Context of the West

From California to Colorado

Half a dozen sweaty men in their thirties pile inside and into the back of a pick-up truck. Over their heads, the Californian sun beats down an intense heat, while the truck climbs steep grades up a fire station road that is often gated at the bottom. No closure today. The group is heading to the summit of the mountain with unusual intentions. The nature of the trek up the mountainside is pleasure, however, everyone in the back of the truck is silent in a manner similar to the calm before the storm. Snuggled in the back of the pick-up truck with the men are their bikes. These are unique bikes, which are like nothing found in bike shops, department stores or distribution catalogues. This is the mid-1970s and these men are summiting Mt. Tamalpais in Marin County, California, the birthplace of the mountain bike.[1]

Mountain bikes were not invented in a study lab or by a group of highly trained engineers. They were developed through a series of tinkering and problem solving by a group of riders in Marin County. These men and women originally created "clunkers," a type of bike meant for dirt roads and trails, differing from the typical bikes of the era. The frames used were vintage Schwinn Excelsior frames from the 1930s and 1940s, which housed a fatter tire than the then-popular skinny road tire. These Schwinn bikes were being set up with a knobby tire made by Uniroyal. The tires were mounted on old steel rims, 26 inches in diameter, which until recent years was the standard size for a mountain bike. Charlie Kelly and Gary Fisher were two of these men making the alterations to the vintage Schwinn bikes. Some modifications came in preparation for the ride, while other parts did not survive the ride down Mt. Tamalpais. Mandatory modifications were made post-ride, after the aging steel components had bent, twisted and snapped.

This evolution of parts left the Marin County riders with fully modified clunkers. In their eyes, this was a large improvement, but the bikes were missing one important change; a new frame would take Marin County from clunker to the invention of the mountain bike. Theses early industrialists in Marin County were literally hands-on in the building and marketing of the first true mountain bike frames. Kelly and Fisher created the company MountainBikes [sic], which built, assembled, marketed and sold early model mountain bikes. Tom Ritchey was their designer and frame builder. Ritchey became a highly regarded name in the mountain bike production industry. The final industry man from Marin County was Joe Breeze. He designed and produced the Breezer (and subsequent Breezer II and III) series bike. This was a true mountain bike frame, which was stronger than any clunker. Both Breeze and his Breezer became inspirations to those building up off-road bikes.[1]

The Marin County builders and their associates had done more than modify bicycles and build frames. They were modifying the bicycle industry and building completely new factions of riders. Before too long, the mountain bike became the most popular style of bicycle in America. Adults traded in their skinny tires for the stability of a "fat tire." Children were upgrading from their BMX bike to a 26 inch wheeled mountain bike. Though not an original intention of the Marin County riders, the face of the bicycle industry was changed.

Fast-forward to the modern era of the mountain bike and change has yet to yield. New trails, companies, stores, and types of mountain bikes are appearing all over the country. Although this may be true in several states and cities across America, it is clearly evident in Grand County, Colorado.

The early days of mountain biking in Grand County were simple. Keith Sanders, a long time local and early arriver to the Grand County mountain bike scene recalls working his way through forest service roads and dirt bike trails. Keith and a few other locals were the first to begin mapping out rides in the Arapahoe National Forest. Keith originally rode a 1987 Miyata Ridge Runner, which was a primitive bike compared to the bikes of today.[2] Soon after getting that first bike, he and another rider named Michael Laporte started promoting the riding scene in the county through the Winter Park Fat Tire Society. Boosterism and the promotion of the Grand County mountain biking scene had officially begun.[3]

Grand County, or more specifically the greater Winter Park area, is the self-proclaimed Mountain Bike Capital USA™. This claim is based on the over 600 miles of trails and two downhill mountain bike parks at local ski resorts. Grand County acts as host to many skiers in the winter months, both Nordic and alpine through the various resorts in the county. The communities of Grand County also provide services for bikers. Bikers of course need rentals and repairs, but are also consumers of food, places to sleep, shopping, and après entertainment.[4]

Tourism in Grand County, Colorado is no new phenomenon. People have been traveling to the Fraser Valley for recreation as long as the roads and trains would allow. Whether it was soaking in the mineral spring in Hot Sulphur Springs, skiing the various ski areas, or enjoying the water system near Grand Lake, in-county tourism has been present for more than a century.[5] Though this is true about generations of tourism in the county, this book is targeted at answering the following questions: How did mountain biking come into existence as part of the Grand County recreational and economic scene? Does mountain biking mirror the trends of the other corporately influenced tourism industry predecessors in the American West or is it an industry with a unique direction?

Mountain Biking and Tourism in the West

Historians in the last twenty years have not neglected tourism in Colorado. The research here finds agreement with much of their work. Annie Gilbert Coleman, William Philpott, and Hal Rothman all have contributed literature on the topic of tourism in the American West.

Coleman's *Ski Style: Sport and Culture in the Rockies* depicts the modern western ski industry as one of glitz and glamour. She portrays western resorts such as Vail and Aspen as places where consumers can purchase an altered (and often times luxurious) experience of a western town combined with convenient alpine skiing. Her depiction of major ski resorts and recreation tourism defines the conflict with ski bum culture and corporate development. As ski consumers of the 1990s and the 2000s indulged in high-end ski areas and enjoyed the surrounding Rocky Mountains, they increased the demands for high-quality accommodations both on and off the slope.[6]

Philpott's *Vacationland: Tourism and Environment in the Colorado High Country* describes the Colorado Rockies in regard to tourism, accessibility to remote destinations, the development of mass consumerism, and the morphing of a place into a product. Philpott suggests that the layers upon layers of tourism blanketed across what he refers to as the "New West" have covered the original scenes, both human and natural. The promotion of the West as a place of tourism and outdoor recreation has overwhelmed the previous identities and created a significantly skewed view of Coloradan life.[7]

Rothman's *Devil's Bargains: Tourism in the Twentieth-century American West* also depicts tourism in the American

West as a region-altering experience; ranch towns and mining strongholds adjusted to a postindustrial society seeking places rather than products. In these places, tourism used to play second fiddle, but once the former primary industries ceased or shrank, tourism took over as the area's mainstay. These transformations were enormous, as not only the economy changed, but also entire places were oddly transformed into "caricatures of their original identities." [8]

Within the development of the ski resort industry, the supporting infrastructures, and the postmodern consumer state of mind, several commonalities can be found with Grand County's mountain bike development. This study of the history and economic development of biking in Grand County parallels the themes of boosterism, consumerism, public lands use, and environmental/recreational concerns, which have long been part of alpine skiing and Colorado/western tourism.

Specifically, Grand County mountain biking tourism associates with the ski industry's focus on quality experiences, as outlined by Coleman. While Grand County mountain biking tourism may not be overly reliant on high-end restaurants, sightings of the rich and famous, or pure decadent luxury, it does carry over much of the expected quality experience the ski industry has fine-tuned. There too is a combination of simple mountain lifestyle and corporately driven experiences, again drawing a likeness to Coleman's ski industry, but expanding on its concepts to include the summer months of a ski town.

Similarly to Philpott's view of the New West, Grand County also finds itself covered with layers of tourism. The newest layer, mountain biking, is growing at an outstanding rate, once again changing the setting of Grand County for a new season and a new generation of outdoor tourists. Grand County's mountain biking industry serves as an additional example of well-branded and packaged adventure activity, sold to the consumer as an authentic experience.

Just as Rothman's *Devil's Bargains* discusses the changing of economies in western towns, Grand County has its own examples of former operational ranches converting to dude ranches. Combined with the region being a mountain bike summer haven, these dude ranches have expanded to create private trails for bikes and host events, taking their "caricature image" to the next level.

In the broader context of the American West, Grand County's mountain biking scene plays into a few prominent themes. First, the amount of public lands incorporated into the Mountain Bike Capital USA™ trail system is immense. From the roots of biking on Forest Service roads to the modern designed trails at Winter Park Resort, issues with public lands usage of the West's past stay true in Grand County. Finding proper ways to use, maintain or preserve the public lands in Grand County is Wallace Stegner-esque. The work and study the federal lands agents put into balancing the public's needs and the environment's needs meshes well with some of Stegner's views on public lands.[9] Also in the ideological realm of Stegner is the sense of individuality people feel when confronting the vastness of the West. Grand County mountain biking feeds into this by providing a place for tourists to experience the West as if they were tackling it from a stereotypically perceived frontiersman's past.[10]

Focusing on the economic history of the American West, Grand County ties in with post-World War II trends from Gerald Nash's *World War II and the West: Reshaping the Economy*. In this, Nash finds the West was in position to change in both encouraging and undesirable ways. With an influx of urban centers and technology, the West was on the cusp of developing a postindustrial economy, including tourism. On the other hand, places in the West such as Grand County soon experienced a continuing decline in cattle and mineral markets, leading to a decline in those in-county industries. With a long history of winter sports recreation and tourism, Grand County's morphing economy has continued its post-World War II trends toward tourism, and more recently, mountain biking.[11]

Summer in Grand County used to be rather sleepy, but it is now an eventful season with several mountain bike race series, festivals, and casual riding galore.[12] This spike in activity has changed the way resorts and the local businesses plan their summers. The use of public lands in Grand County evolves as new land users search for their slice of nature. Organizations have formed in order to foster the new industry. Corporations invest more into a postmodern capitalistic tourist economy, focusing on the selling of experiences, rather than goods.[13] Examining the growth and cultural changes of mountain biking in Grand County gives an applicable insight to other mountain towns in Colorado and across the country.

The cultural impacts of mountain biking, in regards to this microhistory, are the changes Grand County residents have made in their summer living, work habits, and relationship with the outdoors. The tourism industry also shows a cultural change in the way people recreate and the volume at which they do. These changes are measurable in quantitative ways such as sales and taxes, but can be also seen through policy, experience and observation. The development of mountain biking as an economic driver in Grand County exemplifies transformations that are larger than the Marin County clunker builders could have ever of imagined.

2

Technological Advancements and Popularity

Clunkers and Mountain Bikes

The earliest breed of mountain bike was hardly a mountain bike by today's standard. Bike builders in the 1970s were not designing commercial bikes, but were rather making bikes for the purpose of exploring trails and gravel back roads. These bikes were stripped down pre-World War II Schwinn bikes, customized to the rider's delight. Customizations included motorcycle brakes, new forks, handlebars, and tires. The redesigned bikes, "Clunkers" as they were called, were the heavy recycled machines that sparked the interest of cyclists in California and Colorado. Starting with John Finley Scott's 1953 "Woodsie" bike featuring straight bars and knobby tires, mountain bike technology changed little throughout the 1960s and into the early 1970s. By the mid-1970s, tinkerers were putting derailleurs on their clunkers. With the addition of derailleurs, riders were able to change gears, which made the bikes much more trail-worthy than their heavy predecessors. One such builder, Joe Breeze, briefly built bikes for friends in northern California, but by the end of the decade, a manufactured option for purchase was not yet readily available.[1]

Shopping for a mountain bike in 1980 was not the most difficult decision a person could have to make. A consumer shopping for the newly developed bicycle had very few options. Because of the limited supply and even more limited suppliers, the main difficulty would have been even securing a bike. In the most likely scenario, a consumer in 1980 would have bought a MountainBike produced by Charlie Kelly and Gary Fisher in Marin County, California. MountainBike had a stronghold on the market, offered the most up to date equipment on their bikes, and featured frames by designer Tom Ritchey.[2]

The next thirty-five years in mountain biking development proved consumers desired more than just a steel frame, rigid fork and mechanical brake machine of the 1980s. Mountain biking, as a recreational activity, exploded in the

1980s and 1990s, which paved the way for more technological advances and seismic industrial growth. The mindset of the sport also changed, steering national trends toward involving the masses, as well as the differentiation of machines and trails at both ends of the talent spectrum.[3] Mountain biking morphed with mechanical, style and marketing changes nationwide, all of which aided the economic and industrial growth of the sport.

Technological Advancement

The goal of making mechanical changes to mountain bikes seems simple: "make it better." This streamlined philosophy is great, but what exactly is "better?" This age-old question pulled innovators in many directions. Their answers are found in the wide variety of mountain bikes that have been put on the market in the past thirty-five years.

Technological developments in mountain biking are nothing new. Even the earliest inventors were waiting for technology to catch up with their innovative direction. Charlie Kelly and Gary Fisher had to wait for the creation of a properly sized aluminum wheel for their MountatinBike to have correct stopping power. This was common with other bike builders at the time, such as Joe Breeze.[4] In this particular case, the early builders were blessed with the concurrent development of the aluminum rim, which changed mountain bike building in a few (but significant) ways.

First, the wheel was much lighter and shaved several pounds off of the still-weight of the bike. Additionally, the rolling weight of a wheel was found to have a multiplying affect on wheel weight. An accelerating wheel has four times the measured weight of its still-measurement.[5] While this was only additional weight when the wheels were accelerating, in mountain biking this acceleration happens often, as riders navigate slow and unruly terrain. The weight factor alone made the aluminum wheel a huge asset for the early innovators and allowed designers in the early 1980s to get bikes under twenty-eight pounds as well as increase the moving performance of the wheels. [6]

The aluminum rims also changed the way that early bike builders could design braking systems. Mountain bike frame builders and clunker tinkerers could not use preferred cantilever brake systems on the old-style steel wheels that were available in the 26-inch size, which were still being used by default. These riders and builders had to either use coaster brakes, which are built into the crank of the bike, or use modified motorcycle hub brakes. The coasters were a problem because they would burn a lot of grease due to friction and fail on steep or long descends.[7] The motorcycle mods were heavy, and again added to the still weight and even more to the rolling weight of the bike.[8] The aluminum rim fixed this problem by making the cantilever braking system compatible on a 26-inch wheel. Weight was decreased, stopping failure was minimized, and stopping power increased for the next generation of mountain bikers.

The builders and designers of today have a steady stream of change to aid their more contemporary engineering efforts. Technological innovations and improvements, such as aluminum and carbon, can be tracked throughout the 1980s, 1990s, and into the modern generations of mountain bikes. Comparing a spec sheet of a 1980 MountainBike and a 2010 Gary Fisher Superfly 100 (both of Gary Fisher origin), almost every square inch of the bike has seen an innovation in function, material, or comfort.[9]

The modern Superfly is an example of years of improvements compiled into a single bike. Starting with the base, most modern frames now come in choices of aluminum, steel, or carbon fiber. The 2010 Superfly, as well as subsequent models built by Trek from the same decade, have come with carbon or aluminum frames.[10] Carbon and aluminum both have proven better than traditional steel tubing in endurance stress tests.[11] The modern fork, which is the part of the bike that holds the front tire in place and controls the steering, almost always has a suspension system. Third-party companies, such as the Fox Shock found on the 2010 Superfly, design forks for bike manufactures, as well as design aftermarket add-ons. This is enables a bike to be more comfortable than the old rigid steel fork and frame combos, which was the standard through the 1980s and into the mid-1990s.[12]

Braking systems have gone through several transformations, which have led to hydraulic pressured lines and rotor-style disc brakes. These rotor brakes were a play off of motorcycle braking systems, but are much smaller and lighter. They have increased braking power and allow for braking consistency in all varieties of weather conditions.[13]

This specific mountain biking brake technology became so efficient it has recently influenced the road cycling world, which strives on even the smallest advancement in technology. Hydraulic disc brake systems became incorporated into road biking designs in the 2010s. As of April 2015, the road racing sanctioning body, Union Cycliste Internationale (UCI), has allowed for the rotor disc braking systems to be used in professional road races. The technology has proved to be beneficial to cyclists due to the additional stopping power and consistency. The industry-wide acceptance of mountain bike developed technology is evidence of how far mountain bike engineering has come since the late 1970s clunker build-ups.[14]

In addition to the brake system installed on the wheels, the rim sizes have evolved too. Most bike companies expanded wheel and frame designs and are currently offering 26-inch, 27.5-inch, and 29-inch mountain bike rim sizes. The different wheel sizes have allowed for differing feels on the trail and facilitate a variety of skill sets. The standard 26-inch wheel is smaller, more agile, and boasts a tighter turning radius, which is a benefit on tight trails and switchbacks. The 29-inch wheel set, more commonly referred to as the "29er," has been the giant on the trail. The larger wheel size gives the rider an improved approach angle to tackle obstacles on the trail, allowing the biker to ride over items without feeling as much of the impact.

The 27.5, or 650B, wheel size serves as both a stepping stone for riders looking to size up from the standard size, or as a compromise for a rider looking for the best of both worlds.[15] The 27.5 wheel makes fitting bikes easier as well, especially with smaller frame sizes. Fitting large 29-inch wheels on a small or even medium frame can make for a geometric challenge. The 27.5-inch wheel has provided designers and bike fitters with another option to improve the rider's experience.[16] These wheel innovations increased performance and comfort for the rider.

Mountain bike technological innovations are constantly changing and have improved several features of the mountain bike. As a result, parts have been redesigned, replaced by better functioning mechanisms, and built with stronger and lighter materials. Riders, including those living and visiting Grand County, Colorado, have been provided a safer, more comfortable, and better-equipped machine. They have also been given the opportunity to explore more types of terrain at an efficient level as either a first time rider or an experienced veteran.

Technology driving social change is not a new concept in history and particularly applicable here is a version of the theory of technological determinism. As described by Merritt Roe Smith, a "soft view" of technological determinism finds that "...technology drives social change but at the same time responds discriminatingly to social pressures...[17]"

Mountain bike technology fits well into this soft view of technological transformation, as trails and riding styles have followed the advances in technology. Conversely, mountain bike technology has also responded to social pressures by developing in ways that create more comfort and safety for the riders embracing it. This is similar to the changes in the automobile industry when technology increased performance or comfort in a vehicle. As technology advanced in automobiles, new drivers were welcomed into the market. The invention of the automatic transmission opened up roadways to drivers of varying ability.[18]

Technology in the winter mountain sport of downhill skiing has a resemblance to these accommodating technological changes as well. As technology advanced throughout the decades, skiing experiences were altered by increasing accessibility, which ultimately led to more people enjoying the sport.[19] Advances in mountain bike technology are similar in nature to the changes in skiing and automobiles, as modifications have provided riders with higher performing products of leisure and comfort, in place of more primitive designs from the decades prior.

Horizontal Expansion

The evolution of mountain bikes since their debut in the late 1970s is an observable shift. The technological advances, specifically in bike building, have allowed not just one bike to prosper, but have created several subgroups of mountain bikes and merged them into the market. In 1980 there was just plain mountain biking. A rider had one style of bike, set up to ride on trails and explore dirt roads. The 1980 bike had to ascend steep uphill, descend rugged downhill, and travel the flats in a fairly efficient manner. The advances in technology helped those all-mountain bikes become more efficient. Though technology did help the original mountain bike in terms of comfort and safety, the new technology also pushed the sport of mountain biking to expand into subgenres.

Considering the modern USA Cycling categories in mountain biking, it is evident the sport has evolved horizontally, meaning that a wide spectrum of riders now participate in various styles of riding. Each of these disciplines showcase different skillsets of riding. Cross-country riding, which is most similar to the original styling of the sport, consists of longer distances, climbing, and some rough terrain. Downhill riding is a genre of riding that consists of taking ski lifts or shuttle buses to the top of mountains and speeding down through a set course consisting of bumps, jumps, rocks, and drops. Enduro riding combines the two aforementioned ends of the spectrum and requires rider to climb to check points and race the downhill portions. There are also recently added collegiate and high school championships, of which USA Cycling oversees.[20] This does not take into account, however, the assorted styles of freeriding disciplines that have become popular in the past few decades.

Diverse styles of mountain bikes are now available to support these specialized styles of riding. These bikes developed over time, in conjunction with the proper technologies. All of the differing styles are still considered mountain biking, but the bikes are vastly different from each other. These alterations are most apparent in the suspension systems, the geometry, and the weight of the bikes.

With all of these different types of mountain biking and the technology to support them, the mountain bike industry has expanded. This growth is evident from the larger selection of mountain bikes companies now have in their catalogues. Specialized, for example, as of 2016 had seven full suspension bikes they manufactured. This was in addition to the six hard-tail (front suspension only) offerings. In 2002 the company only had five mountain bikes total, two of each style, and one with an optional rear suspension.[21] The growth of technology and innovative bikes created a market in which experienced riders pushed the limits on high-tech bikes, whipping down seemingly impossible trails, while the new riders to the sport propelled a modestly equipped bike across town on local gravel bike paths in complete comfort.

Bike resorts and trail designers embraced these expansions through the development of trail systems, which host many of these different subgenres. Winter Park Resort, for example, is home to a large downhill and enduro biking infrastructure and scene.[22] Granby Ranch, also in Grand County, maintains a slightly smaller downhill mountain bike park. As these subgenres of biking evolved, the features and terrain at these facilities have as well. Other resorts, such as Devil's Thumb, and Snow Mountain Ranch host various forms of mountain biking as well, which exemplifies how the many levels of mountain biking has infiltrated the county. With additional types of bikes on the market and numerous types of riding to do, mountain bikers in Grand County began to buy more bikes. It is not uncommon for a modern-day mountain biker to own more than two or three specialty mountain bikes.[23]

Prices and Purchasing Mountain Bikes

The pricing of mountain bikes has also allowed for the industry to grow. Bikes have improved in quality, variety, and technology while decreasing in relative costs. Once again referring back to the 1980 MountainBike, the consumer would be facing a price tag of $1,300.00, which converts to $4,121.62 in 2017 buying power.[24] A trail-equipped mountain bike today, which could withstand a similar ride to the 1980 MountainBike would cost significantly less. A comparable modern trail bike is the Giant ATX 27.5. Looking over the specifications for the 2017 Giant, it rivals or exceeds any part of the 1980 technology, including larger wheels, front suspension, and disc brakes. The retail price of the 2017 ATX 27.5 was $450.00.[25] This price difference has made it easier for the modern consumer to purchase a trail-equipped bike and has expanded the market to include more riders.

Pricing of mountain bikes in the early days of the sport were high due to the individualized craftsmanship that went into each bike. When Gary Fisher, Charlie Kelly, and Joe Breeze were building bikes, the frames were hand-built by local American manufacturers. A builder, such as Tom Ritchey, was not a cheap source of labor. His time building frames and forks was expensive and he was relatively slow as a bike builder compared to industrialized machining and factory labor. Early builders also had to find correct mountain bike parts and components and assemble the whole bike. This led builders on a chase through distributors and shops for worthy componentry. Fisher and Kelly often performed these tasks themselves or assigned the job to the few employees they had.[26]

This all changed when Mike Sinyard started his bike supply company Specialized. Sinyard's company was one of the original suppliers for MountainBike and he caught wind of their innovative bike building operation. He had his own ideas on how to bring mountain biking to the forefront of the cycling industry. Sinyard, through Specialized, outsourced much of the bike manufacturing process to Asia. In 1982 he built the Stumpjumper, the flagship model of Specialized, which according to Kelly, was nearly identical to the original Ritchey-engineered MountainBike. The key difference was the cost of the building and assembling process, which was far less expensive and could be done at a higher volume.

The mass outsourcing of mountain bikes had begun. Other companies began to follow this trend. Two companies, Univega and Murray, soon produced and distributed high production, economically priced mountain bikes, which provided consumers with more options and significantly reduced prices.[27] These more affordable bikes make up the majority of bikes sold today. In 2015, 73% of bikes sold were from department stores rather than specialty bike shops. Lower priced bikes, such as Schwinn/Huffy/Mongoose parent company, Dorel, sold rapidly through big-box distribution channels. While these bikes made up a majority of the units sold, they were only 32% of the actual sales share of the industry, leaving the balance of the income to sports shops and bike specialty stores.[28]

The more attractive price of mountain bikes has not been the only factor motivating consumers. Companies have broadened their advertising and marketing approaches to include almost all demographics. Mongoose, a popular mountain bike and BMX company, explored early marketing changes in the 1990s. In 1998 they attempted to attract alternative sport enthusiasts with a series of advertisements, which promoted mountain biking to younger riders in the BMX racing scene.[29] The BMX racing and freestyle scene was experiencing a renaissance in the mid 1990s. Expansion of the sport at professional levels, accompanied with major media events on ESPN and NBC, aided in bringing young riders back into the bike-riding scene. This demographic became a focus of mountain bike companies' advertising.[30]

A similar campaign targeting women is a more current happening. Bicycle manufacturers are well aware that women are a large part of the current outdoor recreation industry. They hold much of the buying power in the household and are purchasing more women-specific biking items. Giant, a bicycle manufacturer, has focused on producing more women-specific products as well as sponsoring a race team to promote the sport and their own products specifically to women. Some companies make women-specific bikes at both the high and low ends of production costs. Other companies produce smaller frame sizes of their staple models to entice smaller female riders to purchase. In the 2010s, women are annually responsible for nearly $500,000,000 dollars in women-specific bicycle gear, which has prompted bicycle manufacturers to cater to the growing demographic.[31]

While some companies have focused on producing less expensive bikes, other companies have done the opposite. The high-end bicycle market expanded in the 2000s at a rate of 20% in sales per year. Bike manufacturers Yeti and Titus were among high-end builders who found dedicated bikers were comfortable spending $2,500 to $4,000 on a quality bike. Their marketing has been geared to attract experienced and affluent bikers. They recognized there were seasoned mountain bikers that had ridden for more than a decade and had purchased several bikes. Those consumers were often in search of the best bikes and were willing to pay top dollar.[32]

Mountain bike companies became a part of a wide market in terms of products available and consumer interest. People of both genders and nearly all ages rode bikes with varying levels of ability. Companies noted the broadness of these demographics and responded by differentiating products to fit the market. Growth in women-specific products and high-end bikes in the 2000s indicated mountain biking had grown in popularity and had developed staying power as an outdoor activity and potential economic driver.

Conclusions

Since its inception, the mountain bike industry has experienced myriad technological changes. The ever-changing technology has provided riders with safe and more comfortable machines. Brakes and suspension systems have increased bikes' capabilities on the trail as well as expanded the buying market. The market for mountain bikes range in cost has expanded drastically. Bikes now range from a few hundred to several thousand dollars, depending on where they were built and what types of materials were used. The demographic of mountain bike purchasers has broadened, coinciding with a greater availability of bicycle types. These recently developed demographics and subgenres of mountain biking expanded sales and created niche markets for bicycle manufacturers. The changes in the market turned the sport of mountain biking from a one-company experiment in 1980, to a multifaceted industry with dozens of companies in the 2010s.

The localized impact of this technological boom inside the mountain biking industry is found within the tourism industry's ability to provide more types of riding and more comfortable riding. Local entities and downhill biking facilities have developed and expanded trails based on the technology developed for the mountain bike. This expansion of the industry through technology unlocks a level of comfort and accessibility, acting as a gateway to consumers similar to developments of the ski industry outlined in Coleman's *Ski Style.*[33] The technological advances in fat tire technology have also lengthened the biking season into the winter, providing riders the option to bike in the snow, as well as ranches and resorts an opportunity to market and benefit from the industry, even in the snowy months.

These opportunities for a unique, yet comfortable and affordable experience harmonize with Hal Rothman's capturing of the "third nature" postmodern consumer mindset of Americans in regards to outdoor tourism. Tourists seek experiences and gain a sense of fulfillment by conquering new outdoor activities. While the material bike is an industrial good, it has opened a gateway to non-material experiences, such as exploring the National Forests or riding full-suspension bikes down a ski-slope in July.[34] Even though mountain bike technology may appear trivial or represent more of an overview of industrial change, the local impact to a place such as Grand County come simply as better vehicles for the tourists to explore on.

3

Grand County as a Recreational Space

A Place and a Venue

Most often, sports need a proper venue to be performed. For example, a baseball game has a field for a venue. If the field is intended for youth baseball, it might be a flat corner of a city park. For a small college or high school, a baseball field may have seating for a few hundred people, restrooms, and a concession stand. If a baseball field is intended for a professional team, there will likely be parking lots, elevators, lights, electronic scoreboards, box seats, television studios, and restaurants.

Denver's Coors Field, home of the Colorado Rockies Major League Baseball team, has all of the listed amenities and more. Coors Field has ample parking, with three large parking lots on-site, bike parking, public transportation, and surrounding city parking for up to 46,000 vehicles. There are sixty public restrooms on the grounds. In Section 127, a lost and found system is in place for the convenience of venue users. Lost children are also taken to Section 127, and hopefully reunited with parents. Five elevators serve all levels of the building in addition to the five escalators assisting pedestrians up and down the stadium bowl. Last, but certainly not least, venue patrons have access to forty-nine types of concessions, (not including varieties) which are found in both stationary and mobile locations all throughout the venue.[1] Other major commercialized sports follow this design of a hospitable sporting venue, but mountain biking has different needs in terms of a venue.

Mountain biking venues are places with open areas in which to ride. Riders look for places with trails, scenic views, and physical challenges. Since most mountain bike tourists are participating, rather than spectating, the venues for mountain biking generally do not have bleachers for seating. Mountain bike venues rely on trail access, volume of terrain, and a welcoming atmosphere as a draw for participants. Grand County, Colorado has a long-standing reputation of being a great mountain bike venue, but what exactly has made Grand County such a quality mountain biking venue? The following will assess Grand County as a mountain biking and outdoor recreation venue in terms of sport tourism.

Relative Location

Grand County sits not far from Interstate 70, which serves as the vital artery of traffic infrastructure for Colorado's high country tourism.[2] Head north over Berthoud Pass via U.S. Highway 40 and Grand County is tucked in behind the Continental Divide as parts of the Fraser and Colorado River Valleys. By way of Interstate 70 and U.S. Highway 40, Winter Park, the first town on the descent into Grand County, is seventy miles from Denver. This makes it easily accessible for visitors from Denver to make weekend trips to the county. Well-maintained transport routes, such as U.S. Highway 40 and Interstate 70, are key for sport tourism, especially when a venue is not in a highly populated area. The proximity to Denver International Airport also makes Grand County an easy destination to get to for out-of-state and international travelers.[3]

Access to Grand County was not always such a simple task. Before the Moffat Tunnel opened in 1928 and the year-round opening of Berthoud Pass in 1931, Grand County was often an inaccessible venue for many months of the year. Traveling over Rollins Pass via railroad in the winter months was unpredictable due to high snow volume. After transportation routes allowed for relatively dependable travel to and from Denver, the skiing industry boomed and the status of Grand County as a destination venue strengthened. Trips to the Arapahoe National Forest were an easy day or weekend trip, as compared to traveling further west to other public lands.[4] The automobile and the roads designed after its popularity increased became a medium for tourists to travel to the nearby outdoor venues. Cars offered a way for people to interact with nature and reinforced the bond Denverites had with coming to the Fraser Valley for recreation from the early era of sports tourism. Automobile use now doubled as both transportation machines and a means of self-expression and exploration.[5] Routes such as U.S. 40 and Interstate 70 are rooted in tourism, as their early planning and promotion at the state level was influence by tourism boosters.[6]

This relative location to Denver is important for Grand County as a sports tourism destination. It is not however, located immediately inside the market, which has had a number of positive impacts for Grand County. First, sport tourists traveling a distance tend to respect a time/cost/distance threshold. This means a family traveling will have invested time and traveling costs into a trip. With that investment, they are more likely, obligated in a sense, to entertain themselves through tourist activities, dining out and other happenings they might not typically partake in on a regular basis. The further a tourist has traveled, the more invested they feel in the trip.[7] For example, a family traveling from Denver to Winter Park are likely to go out to a pleasant lunch or enjoy a couple laps on the alpine slide because they have invested their time and travel costs to get to Winter Park. This is evident in a 2012 exit survey from the Epic Single-track Race Series, which is held in Winter Park. The series hosts several hundred racers per event, many traveling from Denver to race. The data, collected after the series was over, showed that nearly half of the racers stayed the night in a hotel or rental house.[8] If they lived closer to the venue and did not feel invested in the travel time/costs/distance to get to Winter Park, this revenue would not have been generated.

Grand County does have a slight disadvantage here, since there are several other destinations farther away. The disadvantage being that people are likely to spend more time and money at the other venues due to increased travel investment. Grand County however, may be frequented more often with a similar sentiment of travel investment.

Grand County: A Peripheral Sports Venue

An important reason why Grand County's proximity to Denver is beneficial is that its slight remoteness defines it as a peripheral destination venue, rather than a centrally located venue. A peripheral venue is a venue based on natural resources rather than traditional sports venues and infrastructure.[9] This is exemplified in Grand County by its variety of ski terrain, white water rafting, hiking, lake recreation, and mountain biking. Even with all of this venue variety, it is not relatively far removed from Denver. Traveling to the western slope of Colorado or up north to Jackson Hole, Wyoming, for example, is a trek, making Grand County an inviting neighbor to the Front Range of Colorado. This perception as a peripheral venue and remoteness combined with a shorter commute, has given Grand County a marketing advantage in regards to sports tourism.

Grand County relies on its local natural resources to draw in tourists. Winter is themed by the snowfall at the ski resorts of Winter Park and Granby Ranch. Grand Lake's winter is also paced by the snowfall due to the snowmobilers flocking to the region. The non-winter seasons rely on several resources; the diversity of Grand County's geography attribute to the variety of summertime activities that occur in the county.

The Fraser River and Colorado River serve as popular rafting and kayaking venues. The towns of Fraser, Granby, Hot Sulphur Springs, and Kremmling all hosts hordes of boaters throughout the summer. In additional to the boaters, the rivers welcome many fishermen. Grand Lake, Shadow Mountain Reservoir, and Lake Granby are home to fishing and recreation boaters alike. Hikers, equine enthusiasts, off-road vehicle users, and mountain bikers enjoy the seemingly endless acres of public lands and other trail systems.[10]

Mountain bikers specifically have an outdoor venue of nearly infinite magnitude. Grand County is recognized for its more than 600 miles of mountain biking terrain. This vast amount of riding is intriguingly large, although peripheral venues are not just about quantity of a resource. A sought after peripheral venue has six specific qualities.[11]

The first quality is that the venue must facilitate access to the participants of an activity attempting to partake in a sport. In nature, it is also ideal to have an infrastructure supporting outdoor athletes.[12] Grand County has secured this quality over the years, mainly at the downhill bike facilities in the county. The ski lifts double as bike lifts in the summer, which is a human infrastructure providing access to nature. Forest Service roads and developed trailheads are a unique type of infrastructure, both of which are of abundance in Grand County. [13]

The second quality of a peripheral venue is the type of participation. Sport tourists in a peripheral venue are normally active participants rather than spectators. In other sports markets it is normal to have spectators travel from out of town to witness an event, but with peripheral venues, people are coming to the venue to race or participate.[14] Coaches and family members often come to these venues to support the athletes, but even they partake in some forms of tourism and generate revenue.[15] Mountain biking in Grand County proves to draw participants to races at Winter Park Resort, Granby Ranch, and Snow Mountain Ranch in addition to the general participants on the trail.

The quality, rather than quantity, of sports in a region is the third attribute of a peripheral venue. The quality of a sport can be determined by the "uniqueness, naturalness, absence of impact, remoteness, and features of the natural environment."[16] Grand County's mountain bike marketing in recent years has often been based around its quantity, however it does maintain a lot of the attributes of quality. The reviews of mountain biking in Grand County are often of the quality, focusing on both resort trails and on public lands trails. MTBProject, a website in partnership with the

International Mountain Bike Association (IMBA), notes that the Winter Park area is abundant in great trails and is home to good trails for people of all styles and all abilities. IMBA projects Grand County as a removed location from Denver and as being a natural scene with trails in river valleys and high alpine surroundings.[17] This reception, as well as others by third-party reviewers, confirms the quality of trails in Grand County meets tourists' standards, which qualifies it for being a proper peripheral venue.

Another property of peripheral sports venues is the clustering of sporting locations. By having clusters of sporting locations throughout a venue, the tourists can more easily access the sporting sites for participation.[18] This makes for a better experience for tourists, as they look to maximize their time visiting. This can be difficult for peripheral sport venues to achieve however, due to the fact that they are natural resources and are not under total human control.

Grand County has been successful in this clustering of venues. Maps of mountain bike trails in Grand County show there are indeed clusters of trails all around the county, but the heaviest concentration is in the Winter Park/Fraser end of the valley. These systems are often four to twelve trails interwoven and sometimes connected by back roads or other trails. These clusters also have amenities such as bathrooms, camping, and parking. Items such as these build clout. Grand County's trail systems are organized, well marked, and are enjoyed as small separate riding zones.

The fifth attribute of peripheral venues is having a service industry and infrastructure available to offer comfort to tourists. This comes by way of lodging, restaurants, and support shops.[19] Grand County has an advantage in terms of services because of the existing winter outdoor sports scene. Skiing has been a part of Grand County for over a century, beginning with the Hot Sulphur Winter Carnival back in 1911.[20] Since then, Winter Park Ski Area opened in 1940, which has ushered in many lodging facilities, restaurants, and workers to serve sports tourists. These changes prompted the facility to change its name in 1985 to Winter Park Resort.[21] The resort now acts as a mountain bike facility in the summer, bringing lodging and service to an outdoor mountain biking venue. The ski industry-based services flip to tend to summertime activity participants. Similar increases in infrastructure at Granby Ranch have improved venue quality in the region.

The final attribute of a peripheral sport venue is a sense of motivation to participate in the sport while visiting the venue. This also includes the urgency a tourist feels to participate while visiting an area. Specific trail systems in

Grand County have a better reputation and therefore are a higher priority than other trails that are either basic or not as exciting. For elusive reasons, some trail systems in Grand County host especially high volumes of visitors, while others, seemingly similar, have lower use rates. Grand County officials in neither case appear to advertise or promote particular trails in lieu of others. The Headwaters Trail Alliance, a non-profit organization in Grand County, is attempting to create a sense of motivation among tourists. They are creating an "epic ride," which is supposed to be a combination of trails in a fifty-mile loop. They intend to promote the trail as a "must-do" in Grand County, thus developing a deeper sense of motivation for tourists to participate.[22] The resorts in the county create their own sense of motivation on their trails through advertising campaigns. Though at first advertisements are openly bias, a genuine motivation to experience a particular trail develops, prompting tourists to seek out certain trails.

This mountain bike boosterism is similar to that in the ski industry. By bundling scenic views, action, activities, and genuine outdoor experiences, ski promoters have created bundles to sell to consumers. Packaged and controlled experiences were designed with town history, charm, and skiing, then were sold to ski consumers.[23] The parallels between winter's skiing and summer's mountain biking are sibling-like.

Grand County fits many of the essential attributes to be sought after as a peripheral sports venue for mountain biking and other outdoor adventure sports. The geography in the county permits tourists to experience various types of nature. Trail clusters across the county act as smaller venues within a larger one. The snow season service industry doubles as a more than adequate summer tourist service industry. Considering these attributes, Grand County has developed into a positive example of an outdoor recreation venue and proves its ability to host tourists looking for quality mountain biking experiences.

Roots to Filling the Seasonal Void

Grand County has a long history of being a seasonal peripheral venue. The county's history of skiing predates the invention of the mountain bike. For eight decades, winter skiing brought tourists to the county to ski in Hot Sulphur, Grand Lake, Granby, and Winter Park before the mountain bike was even invented in California.[24] In that time, the winter months became the main draw for sports tourism in Grand County. Having a seasonal industry comes with drawbacks; Grand County faced typical problems of seasonal peripheral venues.

When mountain biking started becoming popular in pockets across the American West, locals in Grand County caught onto the trend. In 1988, locals Keith Sanders and Michael Laporte started the first community group to promote mountain biking in the county. The Winter Park Fat Tire Society was formed to act as the booster for the new sport and to organize the young local industry.[25]

Winter Park's arrival onto the mountain bike scene came in the same era as that of Fruita, Colorado. The Colorado Plateau Mountain Bike Trail Association (COPMOBA) started in 1989 with trail building and maintenance programs that continue to the present.[26] Though 1988 and 1989 are early in the mountain bike scene, other towns in Colorado were already working on supplementing their summer economies with the revamped two-wheeled contraption. Crested Butte, often considered the first mountain bike town in Colorado, began certain types of off-road riding in 1976, riding Pearl Pass to Aspen. The Crested Butte scene became more solidified and organized with the creation of the Fat Tire Bike Week festival in 1981.[27]

Similarly, The Iron Horse Bicycle Classic started as an exhibition road bike race in 1972, racing a train from Durango to Silverton. The festival grew throughout the 1970s into a pro event. Iron Horse organizers began to include and promote mountain bike racing in 1985, as the sport grew large enough to be included into the festival weekend. Durango then hosted the National Championship races for mountain biking four times in the next seven seasons (1986, 1987, 1989 and 1992).[28]

Peripheral venues experience fluctuation due to seasonal changes, and Grand County is no exception. People come to peripheral venues to enjoy the natural venues that are offered, which often times include the weather in the area. Snow is a fine example of a natural element tourists enjoy. When the snow stops falling and melts into spring and summer seasons, the tourists find other activities to enjoy. Urban venues allow for year-round enjoyment, since they are often indoors. When peripheral venues lose their main attraction, they fail to draw consumers and face the problem of working under a needed capacity to be profitable.[29] Grand County has faced this problem for decades. While Grand Lake offered lakeside activities and access to Rocky Mountain National Park, Granby, Winter Park and Fraser all had far more services available than tourists visiting in the summers. Running at lower tourist levels made for a slow summer season. Many businesses would shut down for several weeks.

According to Keith Sanders, a local Winter Park resident in the 1980s, the traffic was so sparse coming into the county via U.S. Highway 40 that locals hosted in-road bowling outside of Deno's, a local restaurant.[30] Another longtime local, Kery Harrelson, remembered a slow fall in 1996. He and his friends were able to stargaze on a September night in the middle of U.S. Highway 40 outside of the Fraser Brazier. They lay there for about 15 minutes, waiting for a famous carrot dog from the local shop.

In the later 1990s and into the 2000s, these seasonal patterns began to change. Resorts began to challenge their seasonal status by becoming four-season resorts. The larger resort in Granby, Silver Creek, was sold in 1995 for 12 million dollars. The new owner, Antonio Cipriani, began shifting the resort from a ski area to a year-round getaway. In 1998, Cipriani embarked on an 18-hole golf course, complete with clubhouse. By the turn of the century, Silver Creek was expanded through a large land purchase from the federal government and renamed Sol Vista. It was during this period that mountain biking became a part of the business plan for the resort to aide the summer sporting experience. Just a few years later, Sol Vista was once again renamed; Granby Ranch was the new (and current) moniker for the ski and bike resort.[31]

Winter Park Resort also found mountain biking to be a proper fill for the summer and fall seasonal void. Winter Park developed the Trestle Bike Park, which is a lift-served bike park on the ski mountain. Crews at Winter Park began building in 2006, expanding the trail systems to 9.1 miles. The Trestle Bike Park opened in 2008 and has expanded with new trails most seasons following the inception.[32] Trestle Bike Park has brought a new shot of summer life to the base area with riding, races, and festivals.[33]

Conclusions

Grand County has many natural advantages to its location, geography, and weather patterns, which allow it to be a fancied peripheral sport tourist venue catering to Denverites and national tourists alike. Being geographically close to Denver, yet being vastly inverse to the urban lifestyle makes Grand County an accessible and desirable destination. The mix of high alpine, dense forests, and green valleys provide scenic surroundings and variety for an outdoor venue. The snowy winters allow winter sport enthusiasts to enjoy a vast ski/winter venue, while the comfortable arid summers make for pleasant days for mountain bikers and hikers. Grand County has battled the resource-related seasonal difficulties of outdoor venues and has grown in the past decade in terms of capitalizing on the summertime peripheral venues. Mountain biking has been an integral piece of the county's metamorphous from a winter venue to an all-seasons venue.

4

Smokey The Trail Managing Bear

The Sulphur Ranger District Station

Granby is a small town almost in the geographic center of Grand County, Colorado. According to the 2010 Census, it hosts a population of 1,864 people and is the hub for much of the East Grand School District.[1] The high school, middle school, one elementary school, and the small Indian Peaks Charter School are all located in town. Across the Fraser River, tucked away from the local eateries and fishing shops is a United States Forest Service (USFS) station.

The Sulphur [sic] Ranger District serves the greater Grand County region and acts as the heart for all dealings with National Forests and certain protected areas. On a map, the area managed by the station covers the majority of the county. The Sulphur Ranger Districts' managed territory includes a large portion of the Arapahoe National Forest, the Indian Peaks Wilderness Area, James Peak Protection Area, the Never Summer Wilderness Area, and the Vazquez Peak Wilderness Area. The district totals over 442,000 acres.[2] The numerous areas are dispersed across Grand County and each have a unique geographical presence. There are high alpine regions that reach nearly 14,000 feet, dense forests, recently thinned forests due to pine beetles, rolling sagebrush landscape, and lush valleys.

The Sulphur Ranger District manages this land in many facets; they have a broad mission and several responsibilities for the land. The office hosts a plethora of employees and scientists who all have different roles within protection, conservation, recreation, and harvesting of resources. Supervisory Forestry Technician Miles Miller is one of these employees and he specifically focuses on recreation, camping, and trails maintenance.

Miller is a longtime veteran of the USFS and specifically of the Sulphur Ranger District. He has been in Granby at his current post for almost twenty years. This experience, dating back to the 1990s, allowed him to serve through the many changes and trends of Grand County's outdoor entertainment. He has the outward appearance of a man with extensive experience; his white hair, neatly trimmed mustache, and well-worn uniform articles all speak for his years as a USFS Employee. His articulation and knowledge of trail use and recreation on public lands in Grand County comes from years of service, training, and department-led initiatives. Miller detailed his experiences as part of the USFS through an extensive interview, which serves as the foundation of this chapter.[3]

Miller's role in the Sulphur Ranger District is to provide trails and roads across public lands, which grants accessibility to the numerous parcels of public lands for the USFS employees, as well as the general public. Access to land comes in various forms. People drive off-highway vehicles (OHV) onto the public lands to camp and hunt. Hikers walk the many miles of trails to peaks and as through traffic on the Continental Divide Trail. Travelers may use horses and pack animals such as llamas and mules to carry gear into the wilderness. All-terrain vehicles (ATVs) and newer side-by-side utility terrain vehicles (UTVs) travel the national forests with motorized power. In the winter months, snowmobiles explore the depths of the forests on groomed trails and powder fields. Alpine and Nordic skiers cross public lands both mountainous and flat.

In the past quarter century, a new means of exploration and recreation has entered the Grand County public lands: the mountain bike. Miller, along with the district's staff of trail patrol and labor crew, work to manage all the public lands trails and roads for the variety of public users.[4]

Trail Building on National Forests Lands

The USFS currently has to work to maintain much of the mountain bike trail systems, which are spread across the public lands. This has not always been the case. Miller recalls moments of change for mountain biking in Grand County and links the Sulphur Ranger District to several of these changes. In order to facilitate increased mountain bike traffic in the summer months, Miller and the USFS has put forth a conscious effort to create and maintain more mountain bike trails. Grand County mountain biking grew quickly in the 1990s and required a new type of trail. Many early mountain bikers in Grand County rode on Forest Service roads and motorcycle trails, but as the sport grew, the riders began creating their own single track. Miller and the USFS crew had to adapt to the new sport and the miles of trails it was using and creating.[5]

Miller and the Sulphur Ranger District realized back in those early days of mountain biking that it had the potential to become an extremely popular recreation sport and required special attention. They applied more effort in the late 1990s towards creating and recognizing trail systems, which were specifically meant for mountain bike use. Much of the Grand County mountain bike scene took place on USFS maintained public lands and the consensus was that if the USFS did not place an emphasis on building and maintaining trail systems, mountain bike enthusiasts would take it upon themselves to continue to build an excess amount of "user-created trails."[6]

The Sulphur Ranger District's task of limiting new user-created trails has been an ongoing battle since mountain biking's growth in the county. Many of the trails that the USFS maintains are near Winter Park and Fraser. These trails are divided up into several systems. A few of the popular systems, which see high amounts of use are the Idlewild, The Phases, and Experimental Forest trail systems. These systems contain both trails that the USFS created and some user-created trails. Miller and his crew attempt to add new trails and connections annually as needed to keep additional rogue building attempts to a minimum.[7]

User-created trails are a nuisance to the USFS as there are several problems with these renegade trails. First, the trails can be dangerous and poorly built. An amateur trail builder will most likely not create a sustainable and quality trail. Non-sustainable trails lead to erosion problems on the trail, washouts, and irregular water runoff patterns. Second, the trails are not rated or mapped, which can also lead to hazardous scenarios. A person taking an unmarked user-created route may be getting in over their head or lost in an unfamiliar trail system. Even worse, if a rider is injured on a user-created trail, rescuers may not know how to find them. Lastly, user-created routes do not go through the trail creation process, which protects the land from various forms of damage ranging from water, vegetation, and animal habitat destruction.[8]

The process of creating new trails is tedious and resource consuming. The USFS crew cannot add trails wherever and whenever they deem appropriate. There is an office procedure, which takes place by combining the knowledge of several specialists in the local Sulphur Ranger District.

Once the trail crew designs a new route, the proposed route is mapped and sent through the office. Each branch of the office examines the route, looking to see if the trail would impose on the protection or the sustainability of the field in which they specialize. For example, the hydrologist examines a route proposal and attempts to uncover water-related issues that might occur if the proposed route was built as mapped. If the hydrologist deems the route clear of water issues, then it goes on to the next specialist. If there are any potential issues, the trail designer is required to change the route to accommodate the expert's recommendations. This process is repeated with a botanist, habitat specialists, zoologist, biologist, and even an archeologist.[9]

After this extensive internal process, the USFS allows for an external review of the proposed trail. The USFS contacts other invested interests about the trail and includes them in the conversation of the new route. Bike shops, city councils, and adjacent landowners are informed of the new trail and are asked for their input. Similar to the internal process, the trail can be revised to fit the needs of the external input that is provided. For example, if the county office looked over a proposed route and notice a trailside parking area was in the way of a city water drainage area, the USFS has to compromise and adjust. These processes often lead to a proposed trail changing significantly before a shovel is even lifted.[10]

Assembling and Funding Trail Crews

Once an approved trail is built or is in need of maintenance, Miller and his crew physically create, build, and repair them. This typically is a crew of builders working on a new trail, fixing existing trails and clearing downed trees. Over the years, Miller has assembled a trail and road crew that is larger than typical for the Sulphur Ranger District. He has accomplished this largely through the utilization of grant writing. The Off Highway Vehicle Grant Program directly funds two crews working beneath Miller. These crews clear trees in and around trail systems, work on the road and trail conditions, and can even monitor activities on the trails as law enforcement officers. These are both primarily funded by the State of Colorado and, according to Miller, have fostered a positive relationship between the state and federal agencies.[11]

The two grant funded crews are the Statewide Trail Crew and the Grand Lake Trail Crew. The primary function of the Statewide Trail Crew is to visit Colorado's National Forest and Bureau of Land Management (BLM) land and complete assigned projects. Miller is the command for that crew and has them based out of Grand County. They are assigned local Grand County trail projects several times per season. The other state-funded crew Miller is responsible for is the Grand Lake Trail Crew. This is truly a specialized crew. They are a motorcycle-based crew who travel on dirt bikes across all types of trails. The crew consists of four trained riders/chainsaw operators. Packing their chainsaws and trail maintenance equipment, the Grand Lake Trail Crew travels across the National Forest daily and can cover up to one hundred miles of challenging terrain, working on trails while throughout. The bikes allow them to get into various deep country trail systems that may only be accessible by foot or pack animal otherwise. Annual granted funds for these crews have ranged from $175,236 for the Statewide Trail Crew to $99,446 designated to the Grand Lake Trail Crew.[12] This funding covers materials, travel costs, and employee compensation. Miller utilizes both of these crews on the 350 miles of road and 410 miles of trails that the local Sulphur Ranger District is responsible for. He can use them on both motorized and non-motorized trails because he has acquired additional funding through congressionally appropriated funds for non-motorized trail creation, maintenance and law enforcement. Many of these non-motorized trails are the same trails that are being promoted by the USFS and local agencies as premier mountain biking terrain.[13]

The state funded crews are not the only crews Miller has at his disposal. He also has a four-person non-motorized trail crew that focuses primarily on tree removal and trail repair. Additionally, Miller has a two-person travel management crew, which consists of motorized patrol of Forest Service roads, some of which permit access to other motorized and non-motorized trail systems. He has also extended manpower beyond these paid crews by appointing six interns through the Rocky Mountain Conversancy. The interns are in Grand County for seven weeks per season and work on the trails and roads by way of integration with the other trail crews.

These combined trail crews work throughout the summer to keep the trails and road systems on public lands safe. Much of their work includes the removal of trees. Miller estimates the trail crews clear an average of 10,000 trees per year. This is a recently increased number, as the Mountain Pine Beetle killed trees at a rapid rate. This type of beetle is a natural infestation caused by overgrown pine forests, a habitat that Grand County has in large quantities. The Mountain Pine Beetles start by attacking weak and disease-ridden trees, but once those are gone, the beetles spread to healthy trees. In Grand County, the infestation spread for several seasons and killed lodgepole pines in the area.[14] Miller and the trail crews have labored to keep the trails and roads clear of these felled trees. Keeping the trails accessible to the public is a high priority to Miller, but safety is even more important.[15]

Miller is concerned for the safety of the general public on the forest service land. Two specific scenarios have been especially disconcerting in regards to beetle-killed downed trees. First, people can become trapped on forest service roads as a result of a windstorm. A road or trail, previously passible, can quickly become impassible due to newly downed beetle-killed trees. Trapped people typically do not have proper supplies and can face cold temperatures they are not prepared for. During fringe fall and spring months, temperatures can become fatally low at night. Secondly, Miller has concerns about dead trailside trees falling directly on motorists, hikers, and bikers. This type of accident can injure, kill, and additionally strand a trail user in the forest.[16]

To combat these dangerous scenarios, the trail crews employ two types of clearing methods to keep the trails safe and functional. All the crews practice trailside and roadside harvesting as well as more time consuming large-scale harvesting. Trailside and roadside harvesting keep the dead trees trimmed back away from the trail user, which protects them from direct lumber contact. Wholesale harvests clear nearly entire sections of forest, removing all the unhealthy timber and beetle-killed wood. This is practiced in areas that have been overwhelmingly devastated by the Mountain Pine Beetle. These procedures cause trail closures, but the USFS redirects trail users to other trail systems in Grand County during the clearings and harvests.[17]

The USFS recognized the desire for trails and has found ways to get the agency involved. Organizing crews to build, maintain, and keep trails clear of fallen trees has been a large part of Miller's career. Working through the complex process of trail approval and battling user created routes proved to be extra challenges in the USFS trail building undertakings.

Sports Tourism on Public Lands

The effort and focus that Miller and his USFS crews dedicate to the trails keep the forest trails user-friendly, accessible, and most of all safe. The trail systems provide a venue for recreation and sports-related tourism. Miller is well aware of the importance of recreation to the local economy through local spending and he aims to supplement the tourism through trails and access to the local public lands.[18]

Summer recreation in Grand County on public lands has changed over the two decades Miller has been at the Sulphur Ranger District. In the 1990s, summer public lands recreation in Grand County was lower in volume. These tourists were hikers, campers, river users, lake boaters, hunters and off-highway vehicle users. There was a mountain biking scene, but Miller notes the participation was much lower in the 1990s before the boom in the 2000s. He and the Sulphur Ranger District have attempted to facilitate the growth through maintenance and accessibility to trails.[19]

Miller and the USFS in Grand County have facilitated growth without charging fees at mountain bike recreation areas, the only exception being special permits for races or for commercial use. In order to charge a regular fee to the public, such as an entrance or day use fee, the Sulphur Ranger District would be required to develop the trailheads with specific amenities. The Federal Lands Recreation Enhancement Act (FLREA) provides guidelines as to what specific amenities are needed to charge the public for general use. Amenities such as developed camping, running water, parking areas, and staging areas are among the required improvements to request a user fee.

There is one area in the Sulphur Ranger District that has met the criteria of FLREA. The Arapaho National Recreation Area charges a fee for day use or a season pass. In this area, which is part of the large four lake and reservoir system near the headwaters of the Colorado River, the Sulphur Ranger District developed amenities such as bathrooms with running water, campgrounds with electricity and water hook ups, boat ramps to access lakes, and parking lots throughout the complex to permit larger than typical numbers.

While mountain biking is permitted in this fee area, there is not a devoted mountain bike trail system within the Arapaho National Recreation Area. A FLREA-approved mountain bike trail system in Grand County is not out of the question. Miller is cognizant to the amount of funding mountain biking tourism could potentially bring to the local Sulphur Ranger District. He and the rest of the post are always looking for ways to increase revenue and provide better services to users of public lands.[20]

Sports Tourism Conflicts on Public Lands

Recreation and sport tourism on public lands is not conflict-free. Different sports and hobbyists compete for use of particular trails on the same public lands. This conflict is nothing new to mountain bikers. A relatively early report by the United States Department of Agriculture Forest Service from 1996 suggested mountain bikers were not being well integrated into the trail systems across the American West. In this report, seventy percent of the forest managers had received complaints about mountain bikers from other trail users. A majority of issues (41%) reported to managers were conflicts between equestrian users and mountain bikers. Hikers were the source of a substantial number of complaints as well (31%).[21] Miller has come across many of these types of interactions during his career and the USFS has had to facilitate cooperation among the various user groups to host everyone in a best-fit manner.

Common conflicts occurring in Grand County are the trail users' yielding procedures as well as the struggle of managing which users are utilizing the various trail systems throughout different seasons of the year. For example, in the non-snow seasons certain areas in Grand County are closed to motorized vehicle use. This is done for a number of reasons. The trails are designed and built for a particular type of footprint and motorized use could jeopardize the integrity of the trail or the environment surrounding the trail. Another reason is for the experience. Miller understands hikers and mountain bikers are looking for nature, which is associated with peace and quiet. Including motorized users on trails with hikers and mountain bikers may create a less-than pleasurable experience. A few months later, these summer trails have snow season users, which can foster many new conflicts.[22]

A similar situation occurs between equestrian trail users and mountain bikers. According to Miller and Meara McQuain of the Headwaters Trail Alliance, mountain bikers and horseback riders are many times allowed on the same trail systems, but often do not get along while on the trails. These two sources both confirmed that complaints often come from equestrian trail users regarding mountain bikers not yielding for horses or giving proper passing spaces. An equine riding group went as far as to create posters comparing speeding mountain bikes to the speed and profile of a mountain lion. This poster was attempting to project the anxiety a horse feels when mountain bikers speed by a horse in a trail setting.[23] A mountain bike is more likely to spook horses than other forms of loud motorized transportation or foot traffic.[24]

A recent conflict that mountain bikes have become involved with is actually taking place in the winter season. In this case, "fat bikes" are riding on trails that are traditionally open to Nordic skiers. Fat bikes are a modern build of mountain bikes. They have been modified to house wide tires, oftentimes bigger than a typical motorcycle tire. With these four to five inch wide tires, fat bikes can romp around nearly any terrain, including snow. Groomed Nordic ski trails and snow-covered classic cross-country single-track trails are prime for cruising on a fat bike.

The sharing of the trails between these two user groups has led to public complaints received by the USFS. The bikes tear the trail up, leaving it rutted and non-skiable.[25] The popularity of fat biking has increased in the 2010s. Local shops are renting fat bikes, camps and ranches own their own fleets, and the Winter Park Chamber of Commerce has recently began advertising the activity as part of its campaign to promote the mountain biking scene.[26] Miller has dealt with the growth of fat bikes over the past few seasons, but with more locals riding bikes and more shops renting fat bikes in the winter, a potential resolution could be necessary for the trail users to remain happy and for tourists to continue to come to the area for both bike and ski recreation.

Conflict resolution during times of tension has come in a variety of forms for the USFS. The agency has the choice of whether to keep a trail system integrated or begin to segregate users to separate systems. They control and maintain 410 miles of trails with an additional 350 miles of roads, which give them plenty of choices to designate trails to groups of users. The main objective in these resolutions is maximizing trail use and public lands recreation, increasing the overall amount of sports tourism in Grand County, which in the long run brings additional tax revenue to the county.[27]

Conclusions

Miller and the USFS employees in the Ranger Sulphur District have been devoted to the promotion of public lands use and recreation. As the popularity of mountain biking has increased over the past few decades, the Sulphur Ranger District's focus on mountain biking trail systems and venues has increased concurrently. Miller and his associates balance the growing usage of trail systems and recreation areas with the protection of the land they are managing. This delicate balance to sustain the land and provide outdoor experiences for the public takes specialists of all kinds. As the sport of mountain biking evolves into the winter months, the USFS staff in Grand County have more trails to maintain and more usage decisions to make. Miller expects mountain biking to continue to be popular in Grand County. The projected growth has prompted the USFS to facilitate the sport on public lands in an effort to support public lands use and the local economy via sport tourism spending and tax revenue.

5

Promoting Trails and Connecting Islands

Developing Trails For All

There are trails in Grand County for almost any type of use. People can walk and run the trails, use a type of human-powered mechanism such as a bike or skis, use animal assistance with horses or pack animals, or fuel up and drive various off-highway vehicles (OHV) on the trails. Some trails are looked after and maintained by government agencies, such as the United States Forest Service or the Bureau of Land Management. Other groups in the county complete the various needs of the trail system, such as promotion and public relations. The Headwater Trail Alliance (HTA) is a non-profit advocacy group, which focuses on promoting, maintaining, and actively connecting hiking, skiing and biking trails in Grand County.[1]

HTA has not always existed mainly because there has not always been a need. The demand for a group to do such work developed over the decades since mountain biking's inception. As mountain biking evolved into a sport in Grand County in the later 1980s and throughout the 1990s, various community members took note and formed groups attempting to harness the potential economic driver and organize the activity.

Winter Park Fat Tire Society

The Winter Park Fat Tire Society, better known as FATS, was the first mountain bike focus group in Grand County. Formed in 1988, FATS started developing the trail system in the Fraser River Valley. FATS utilized a byproduct of the logging industry; Forest Service roads and logging trails were linked together to create mountain bike trail systems. This organization, founded by Keith Sanders and Michael LaPorte, served as a central command of sorts for the infant mountain bike industry.[2] Sanders and LaPorte realized there were hundreds of miles worth of proper mountain bike trails in Grand County and sought to make it a summertime industry.

In the early days of FATS the objective was to make mountain biking a popular sport and develop it into an economic driver of its own. FATS attempted to reach this goal by focusing on three areas of work: marketing/public relations, trail system building/maintenance, and through the organization of mountain biking events.[3]

Mountain biking was rapidly rising in popularity in the 1980s as bike manufacturers were outsourcing to Asia. By 1983, most major bike manufacturers had mountain bike offerings. This was a drastically different marketplace than 1981, when MountainBikes had a strong hold on the bike building industry.[4] In 1988, Grand County and FATS reached out to the new participants in the sport, promoting the county as a destination to enjoy mountain biking. Marketing this new venue to potential consumers was uncharted territory for FATS simply because the sport was undeveloped.

To reach their already existing winter outdoor enthusiasts, FATS advertised in the spring and summer editions of popular winter sport magazines *Ski* and *Snow Country*. These advertisements were grouped in with other mountain bike communities located across the nation. Winter Park was described as a bike friendly town, where tours, festivals, and races filled the summer months. Dates and contact information were also crammed into the short advertisement, which usually included a picture of a rider climbing a peak.[5] [6]

In *Ski,* the advertisement was paired with a summertime special article focusing on biking in ski country, which acted as a ten-page insert in the middle of the magazine. These authors wrote about their experiences biking in the mountainous ski towns across the country. Notes and columns described various destinations. Winter Park was right in the mix with other prime riding locations such as Bozeman, Crested Butte, Vermont, and Moab.[7]

FATS utilized the press as a valuable means of promoting Winter Park and Grand County as a premier destination for mountain biking. An article printed in 1988 in *NewsOK,* an Oklahoma news source, demonstrated exactly what FATS was accomplishing in terms of promotion. Winter Park and Crested Butte were both described as destinations with full mountain bike amenities. Bob Colon, the author, brought mountain riding to life, recounted his recent trip to Winter Park and his experiences on the trails. He mentioned FATS and the development of the town and projected a progressive mountain bike resort town and even encouraged fellow Oklahomans to visit.[8]

These examples of marketing and public relations are telling of FATS' direction. First, they reached beyond the local and regional media and expanded to national outlets. This implies that FATS considered Grand County a national caliber destination and promoted it as such. It also indicates FATS was intending to bring more people into the county as tourists, rather than simply converting the locals over to the sport.[9] FATS included locals and encouraged riding locally, but in terms of advertising and public relations, they went after the outside consumer, just as the local ski industry had been doing for decades.

The trail system in Grand County utilized by FATS was a series of old forest service roads and dirt bike trails. An early goal for them was to map and maintain those trails. Having a high quality trail system was essential to making Grand County a mountain bike destination. This seemed simple, but in reality the task was overwhelming. According to Sanders, early trail maintenance of all types, more often than not, fell into the hands of FATS. This was due to the lack of a multiuse trail organization in the county. If there were trails damaged from weather or motorized vehicle use, it was often assumed FATS would take care of it.[10]

This extra burden of trail maintenance lessened in the 1990s as the Fraser Valley Partnership for Trails (FVPT) emerged. The FVPT continued the mapping and maintenance of the trail systems, but was multiuse-focused, involving more stakeholders to support work on hiking, Nordic skiing, horse, and even some motorized use trails. Though the FVPT took over much of the physical work and funding for maintenance, the group was not a visionary group; the FVPT did not expand trail systems or create new connections across the county. They cleaned trails, groomed trails, put up signs, built bridges, and generally kept the status quo in tact. In later years, the FVPT took on expansion projects, as well as started the HTA. Both the HTA and the FVPT were still in existence as of 2017.[11]

FATS' final major contribution to early mountain biking was acting as the facilitator for mountain bike events. Races were held in Grand County starting in the late 1980s and continuing into the 2010s. The King of the Rockies race, created back in the late 1980s, has been incorporated into the Winter Park Resort Epic Singletrack race series, and continues to run every August.[12] Group rides for locals were also organized, strengthening the early bond within the Grand County mountain biking community. Providing events and races for mountain biking constructed a purpose for promotion within Grand County as well as in other mountain bike communities.[13]

Essentially, FATS acted as a "booster" or "promoter" as defined by William Philpott in *Vacationland*. Mountain biking was not just developed for the locals, but was branded and advertised to others across the country. Early boosters in the 1940s did similar work to draw in skiers to the mountains in a comparable fashion as FATS did nearly fifty years later.[14]

Once the FVPT and the HTA were started, FATS was nearly irrelevant. They no longer needed to maintain the trail systems, as there were two multiuse focused groups on the scene. In 1996, FATS dissolved and turned over promotion and planning to the Chamber of Commerce in Winter Park and Fraser, which was carried out by the FVPT. In the midst of this changeover, the HTA eventually became the premier organization for mountain bike development and promotion in the county.[15] The torch of promotion had officially been passed to the next booster.

Headwaters Trail Alliance: Maintaining and Planning

In the early days of the HTA, the group focused on maintaining the status quo. The then-present state of mountain bike growth was expanding at such an expedient rate that the task of organizing was difficult enough, let alone considering further developments. Simple maintenance projects were often the primary focus of the HTA. At the turn of the twenty-first century, however, the HTA began expanding their role in the Grand County mountain bike community. The HTA took to a more visionary approach in terms of the trail networks and shaping the local mountain biking industry. This visionary effort was twofold: HTA efforts were geared toward both the economic growth of mountain biking as a summer industry and expanding the physical venue of Grand County.[16]

The HTA visionary focus in terms of economic growth for the community in Grand County was an effort to harness a new sport and turn it into an economic driver. This transition was similar to that of the development of the commercial ski industry in the 1950s and 1960s. During this era, skiing saw an influx of technology, a rise in popularity and corporate involvement. These three elements shifted skiing from pastime to a standalone economic driver.[17] HTA found mountain biking to have these similar elements and dedicated itself to a comparable development of mountain bike tourism.

The task of creating a mountain bike-based summer economy has been no small mission; the HTA has found it to be decades of work. The first step was finding the communities within Grand County that were accepting of the economic shift and cultural change. Not all townspeople welcomed mountain bikers in the same ways as others.

Kremmling, for example, has less devoted mountain bike trails than nearly the rest of the county, but prides itself on the OHV trail systems and the white water river sports developments it made in the past. The BLM Kremmling Field Office is responsible for much of the public lands in the area and has allocated resources to other areas of outdoor recreation. Their grant application from 2013 demonstrated their devotion to outdoor recreation beyond mountain biking. The grant requested $80,000 of a $120,000 budget for trail and road maintenance on BLM land, which was designated for OHV and all-terrain vehicle (ATV) routes.[18] The application was marked for mountain bike trail maintenance however, there were limited mountain bike specific routes near the town, implying the funded routes were intended for shared motorized and non-motorized traffic.[19] Though the HTA is a multiuse organization, the potential for non-motorized trails in the Kremmling region has not been fully explored in association with the BLM.

Beyond the shortage of trail infrastructure, Kremmling also lacked basic mountain bike amenities. Until 2016, Kremmling was without a bike shop. Prior to that, the closest bike shop was in Granby, twenty-eight miles east on U.S. Highway 40. Neither the Chamber of Commerce nor the BLM office has developed accessible mountain bike specific maps, which has made it more difficult to navigate trails and trailheads in the western section of Grand County.[20] A deficiency of facilities and amenities abetted the failure to gain the interest of mountain bikers, as well as the other supporting trail groups in the county.

On the other end of the valley, the mountain bike has been embraced much more significantly. HTA recognized these early efforts to incorporate mountain biking into the economy and has shifted their focus on continued development of the Winter Park and Fraser area. The Chamber of Commerce of Winter Park and Fraser has actively funded and promoted mountain biking in its respective regions. In more recent years, funding from the City of Winter Park, Fraser, and their joint Chamber of Commerce have helped create a rise in summer-month tax revenue. Another considerable part of this revenue increase was the construction of the Trestle Bike Park at Winter Park Resort. These increases in sales tax revenue in 2009 through 2012 justified the chamber's decision to increase funding for promotion and mountain bike related event hosting by the cities.[21]

Winter Park had increased their spending for the Mountain Bike Capital USA™ campaign, which was a complete facelift to the city-funded mountain bike promotion. They increased the marketing budget and related materials for mountain bike promotion to $75,000 per year. The joint chamber also provided the HTA with an office in Fraser.[22]

The HTA took note of these changes in funding allocation and has since been working closely with the government entities to keep increasing revenue through positive trail design, a visitor center, bike wash station, trail maps and research data. The HTA has also conducted research on what the cities in Grand County can do to better host mountain bikers, and as of 2015, this data was being condensed into an expansion proposal entitled the Master Trail Plan.

The original Master Trail Plan was developed in 1995 with hopes of maintaining and expanding trails.[23] The plan was tweaked occasionally, but had not seen a complete overhaul in twenty years. Inspiration for updating the Master Trail Plan was initiated by observing other mountain bike communities across the country. Keith Sanders and Meara McQuain of the HTA, as well as past HTA employees have been working on the updated plan for several years. Data in other mountain bike destinations showed a small amount of development and concentration could go long way in terms of long-lasting effects for local economies.

A prime example cited by the HTA duo was Fruita, Colorado. The western-slope town invested into several mountain bike trail systems and promotions around 2000 and saw increases in sales tax revenue. From 1999 to 2004, the tax revenue increased by 51%, with larger gains in revenue from restaurants at 80%.[24] Sanders provided similar statistics for the other cities, such as Leadville, and considered them influential to the HTA and their pursuit of a revised Master Trail Plan.[25]

Sanders concluded Grand County could be able to bring in a potential $100,000,000 in total revenue annually if the updated HTA Master Trail Plan is executed properly.[26] Recent tax revenue trends from 2007 through 2015 proved increases in summer spending were possible, even though the winter months were in a several year recession during the same time period.[27] These fiscal trends can be traced to the growth of mountain biking as a sport, a centralized effort to promote recreation tourism, the opening of Trestle Bike Park at Winter Park Resort, and the development of the smaller bike park at Granby Ranch. These have all combined to produce a strong economic driver with even more potential for growth.

Working with communities that have embraced mountain bike culture and welcomed the economic shift has been a success for the HTA. Other cities, such as Kremmling or Granby, which had previously showed considerably less interest in building a mountain biking economy, have shifted to later stages in development within the Master Trail Plan.

Connecting the Islands

During the development of Grand County mountain biking, the communities in Grand County were distinct. Winter Park seemed a world away from Kremmling, just as Grand Lake was different from Granby. A large part of these differences came from the geography of the county. Snow peaks and rivers of the east made for a seemingly opposite place than the rolling hills, sagebrush and ranch land of the central and western region of the county. McQuain and Sanders of the HTA referred to the communities as "separate islands" within the county. The places were unique and separated by vast spaces and wilderness. Both uniqueness and geography have been obstacles to tackle when implementing the economic change of mountain biking tourism.

Connecting the islands in Grand County comes in light of the HTA's visionary approach to mountain biking as an economic driver. The HTA attempted to physically connect the towns of Grand County through singletrack trail. This effort has had both successes and struggles in the past, making the project a work in progress as of 2018.

Successful linkages in Grand County have allowed riders to put together long "epic rides," which may be up to fifty miles or more and take a majority of the day. This type of ride can be often times broken up with meals or activities. For example, a rider could ride from Winter Park to Granby, eat lunch at local Mad Munchies Deli, and make their way back to Winter Park in time for an evening concert in the park and dinner at Cooper Creek Square.

The connections, however, stop there. Mountain bike routes beyond Granby to Hot Sulphur, Kremmling, and Grand Lake do not exist without a considerable amount of riding on highways or county roads. The HTA would even like to see trails of some sort link Winter Park to the top of Berthoud Pass on the southeast end of the county, a project dubbed the Seven Mile Trail. The projected continuation of trails to Grand County towns in all directions would allow mountain bike tourists to expand trip plans and add more of a "must-do" motivation for bikers.[28]

A model example of a must-do epic ride is the Kokopelli Trail in Colorado and Utah. This trail system was developed through connecting a series of BLM roads, singletrack trail, with a few county road connectors. This point-to-point trail spans from Loma, Colorado to Moab, Utah. The entire trip crosses 142 miles of mountainous terrain and desert lands. It can be traveled over the course of several days, as developed campsites serve mountain bikers and hikers alike. Road access creates contact with rider support, emergency vehicles and early cut off point options.[29]

The HTA of Grand County has tried to create a trail of similar nature, but has failed to do so as of yet. Difficulties connecting the islands of Grand County fall back on the vast land being covered and the agencies responsible for that land. Reaching across Grand County would involve crossing BLM land, United States Forest Service land, Rocky Mountain National Park, Colorado State Wildlife land, multiple resorts, and private land. Though most of these entities have agreed on the big picture, working through policies and interagency protocol has developed hang-ups. The HTA has tried to gel these groups into a cohesive force, but has struggled with the differing definitions of trail building and summer tourism.

Conclusions

Trail development in Grand County did not happen on its own nor did it happen overnight. Winter Park Fat Tire Society began working on mountain bike trail development in the late 1980s, before the sport was a clear tourist draw for the county. As mountain biking became more popular, the Headwater Trails Alliance in Grand County placed a special interest in the development of mountain biking as a summer economic driver. They have pushed the sport to grow by expanding trails, making existing trails better, and through productive trail materials, such as maps and signs. The HTA continues to build and expand by attempting to connect the towns and trail systems of Grand County. The organization, which aims to increase tourism, has met obstruction through the nature of the county's physical layout and multitude of public lands policy, as well as resort and private land communication. As the HTA promotes and implements the updated Master Trail Plan, mountain biking summer tourism is expected to grow, solidifying it as a mainstay economic driver for the summer economy.

6

Signs of Cultural Shift

Adventure and Adjustments

Grand County used to be an "Island in the Rockies," as popularized by Robert Black. The county was isolated in the late 1800s as consistent year-round railroad access did not come through the Moffat Tunnel until 1928, and Berthoud Pass did not open year-round for automobile access until 1931. While transportation to the county was available in the summer months, the winters were often times of isolation.

During the era before widespread travel to and from the county, ranching was the way of life in the county. As travel increased, so came the tourists. By 1967, tourism was statistically more gainful than ranching for the first time in the county's history. Tourism brought in 3.4 million dollars in comparison to that of ranching's 3.27 million dollars. Much of this was due to the growth of skiing on Berthoud Pass and at Winter Park Ski Area.[1]

In the decades since, ski season in Grand County has been a primary economic driver. Winter Park Resort and Granby Ranch are the two downhill ski areas, which provide the county with an annual influx of winter tourists. In addition, Nordic skiing, also known as cross-county skiing, became a larger presence in the county with several maintained trail systems, two winter resorts, and a series of backcountry trails. Tax records for the past decade indicate that the ski season made up the bulk of the annual income and accounted for the top revenue months in the local economy.[2] This recreation-based ski culture and subsequent industry took time to develop, expanding from the roots of early skiing as a form of transportation in several towns across the county in the 1880s. In-county skiers began skiing for recreation not long after. [3] This emergence of sport skiing dawned a new economic driver for the county; ski lifts and recreation areas have dominated tourism in Grand County ever since.

At the dusk of the twentieth century, mountain biking emerged in a similar fashion. The sport developed a popular following and became an instigator of change in Grand County. The local and regional culture adjusted in many ways, facilitating mountain bike growth as a sport and as a local economic driver.

The People of Grand County

Grand County of the later twentieth century became home to a largely adventurous population. Skiers, river rafters, kayakers, hikers, and bikers had made Grand County an observably exciting place to live. Transplanted locals, along with Grand County natives, could be found at places such as the Winter Park Pub, sharing stories over post-adventure brews. Kayak runs on the Fraser River, backcountry skiing on Berthoud Pass, or mountain biking Tipperary trail would all be fine conversation starters on the patio of the local bar. Though this may seem trivial, it is actually telling of the Grand County population, similar to fishing tales being told in Boston Harbor, or golf banter in the clubhouse after the conclusion of a great round. Adventure sports, or simply adventure, was a major draw to people moving to and staying in Grand County. These people moved to, live and work where they wanted to recreate.[4] [5]

Local songwriter Andy Straus, an Ohioan transplant who moved here in 2002, is exemplary of this trend. He captured the essence of the local adventurous spirit in his regionally popular song "Et Wah." According to Straus, he receives praise for the song from many locals as it accurately describes why they chose to live in Grand County. The first verse and refrain are as follows:

"There's a kid in me I get to see almost everyday.
I moved to the mountains so he could go and play.
Sometimes it's sunny, sometimes it snows so hard.
There's always something to do in my backyard.
[refrain]
I got fishing. Nothing to do, I got fishing.
I got skiing, on a powder day, I got skiing.
I got drinking, with some good friends and the beers are cold.
I got thinking, this is the best damn way to grow old, Et Wah!"[6]

These transplanted people, from both in and out of state, are an important group of people to have in a tourist town. They certainly did not move to the High Rockies to become full-time tourists, yet they enjoy the land as the tourists do. This relocated, adventurous population in Grand County may not be tourists, but they helped push mountain biking along as a tourist industry within the county.[7]

The importance of this risk-taking demographic was two fold. First, they moved to the county, often buying homes or renting, both contributing to the local real estate market.

Second, and more influential to mountain biking, the large influx of adventure seeking people acknowledged mountain biking as a sport, an industry, and a potential local economic driver. Without a welcoming local population, sport tourism would have been half-hearted. If only the financial sector was striving for successful bike tourism, the new industry might not be cohesive to the local economy. With a participating local population, financial gain was a priority to those invested with additional supports from public passion and enjoyment. Grand County, especially Winter Park and Fraser, were home to many of these supportive, passionate facilitators, giving mountain bike tourism a good place to develop.[8]

Signs of Grand County having a relatively advanced level of acceptance of mountain biking culture were apparent in several ways. An early precondition was that the transplanted population moved to Grand County in search of a place to obtain an adventurous style of living. This winter migration had been happening for decades in the ski scene, but would often result in a mass exodus as the winter season came to an end. Now with an adventurous mountain biking lifestyle and service jobs continuing into the summer, many of these once-seasonal employees have turned into permanent residents.[9] Some individuals even enjoy mountain biking season more than the ski season, even though they moved here for a ski town lifestyle. These locals forgo purchasing a winter pass for skiing and instead invest in a summer bike pass and choose to live near bike trails in the Arapahoe National Forest.[10]

Another sign of acceptance of mountain biking was local and long term transplants becoming involved in the sport. Surely, many mountain bikers transplanted to Grand County, but several Grand County-raised and longtime citizens had not biked prior to the mountain biking movement's arrival in Grand County. This conversion of non-bikers to mountain bikers assisted the creation of a strong mountain bike community.

An example of this changeover is as follows. Tabernash local Maggie Keller moved to the county in the late 1990s and was not a mountain biker when she arrived. She skied and hiked, and then later found biking to be a great additional outdoor activity that fit her lifestyle. Since, she has relied more heavily on mountain biking, as it proved to be less impactful on her body, which allowed her to enjoy the outdoors without significant amounts of knee pain. Snow biking in the winter even allowed her to enjoy the snow when skiing was too hard on her knees.[11]

Previously existing sports tourism, adventurous spirits, local buy-in and embracement of mountain biking created a sturdy foundation for the future summer economic driver. With this foundation solidifying in the mid-to-late 1990s, Grand County has followed a pattern of growth, morphing mountain biking into a mainstay of summer recreation.

From Ski-Town to Mountain Bike Capital USA™

Beyond local participation and buy-in, several modifications and accommodations came in the wake of mountain bike tourism. Today, many of these changes are visible in the cities of Grand County. Various changes were subtle, hardly even noticeable at the time, but demonstrate a genuine shift in the mindset of the people in the communities. Other changes were large life-changing reformations, such as complete retooled business plans to find a niche market in Mountain Bike Capital USA™.

Signifiers of cultural shift from ski town to a summer bike town appeared in both the county's infrastructure and local business practices. Small changes, such as additional bike racks in public spaces and shopping centers, were functional to the communities, since there were an increased number of bikers. Bike racks also sent a welcoming message to tourists. The tourists and their bikes were, in a sense, greeted by Grand County. Hotels and condos also provided plenty of bike rack space available to be used by incoming tourists.

Another inviting gesture signifying a cultural shift was the addition of bike wash stations around the mountain bike communities of Grand County. A bike wash is simple in design: a hose, a water catch or trough, maybe a scrub brush of some sort and rags for drying, grouped together for a basic cleaning of a bike after a muddy or dusty ride. When driving through Winter Park, Fraser, or Granby, one can spot this added feature on the side of bike shops, hotels, and condos. The Headwaters Trail Alliance installed a bike wash station at its headquarters in Fraser and continues to see use from tourists and locals alike. Subtle accommodations, in this case bike racks and wash stations, gave Grand County additional mountain bike attributes. These differences created a unique mountain bike place, most likely differing from the tourists' hometown, offering a safe and hospitable mountain bike cultural vibe.[12]

Various mountain bike signage in Grand County also appealed to mountain bikers, as well as demonstrated expanded embracement of mountain biking in the community. Signs from both the governmental and private sectors were put up around the county on roads, trailheads, on trails, and near points of interest. These signs made the trails increasingly rider-friendly, which was an important modification, as being lost in the woods on a bike in the Arapaho National Forest would be a poor use of vacation time. Beyond these directional signs, the county has placed substantial branding and image signage around the communities. These posters included the retooled Mountain Bike Capital USA™ logo, lists of events, race dates, and maps of local public trails.[13]

Private signs around the community directed tourist attention to mountain bike services and rental shops. The presence of bike shop and resort rental fleets, which have been typically on display on the sidewalk or in storefronts, made a tangible advertisement for sport shops. Several of these fleets are now present on U.S. Highway 40 running through the county. Beside bike shops, restaurants and shopping centers have lured bikers in with welcoming beer banners and easy access biker friendly patios with food specials posted.[14]

Before the mountain bike boom, traveling across Grand County would have been a fairly similar sight to the current post-boom layout. Many of the local service oriented businesses were already built and located in a similar spot in relation to their current location. One aspect, however, would have been different. Numerous businesses would have been likely closed for weeks or even months of the late spring and early summer. The off-season in ski towns, or locally referred to as "mud season" or "shoulder season," was the perfect time for the local service industry to close up shop. Families and employees went on vacations or even simply just closed down for a while to take a break and change over products and menus. With mountain biking tourism on the rise through the 1990s and increasing more in the 2000s, local Grand County shops have changed these business practices. This change was not a simple one to make; families would change the way they lived to better serve and capitalize on the increased biking tourism scene.[15]

Many sport shops, which previously had taken a seasonal break, shifted their business plans to stay open in order to accommodate the early season biking that takes place in May. Evolving ski shops have begun to take time in April to change the shops over to bike shops. Several of the shops started maintaining a rental fleet, as well as a repair center and full inventory of accessories. Icebox Sports in Fraser, for example began practicing this changeover and continues it today.[16] A visitor to Grand County in April or May now had a place to stay, restaurants to eat at, and could leave town with a complete mountain bike outfit. Seeing bikes in April also reminds tourists mountain biking season is near and Grand County is all set to ride. Of course this is not universal, as some businesses in Grand County have continued to take mud season to remodel or take time off.

The towns in Grand County also changed the way in which they operated. Recognizing the rise in summer traffic, tax revenue, and visual bike traffic, cities began developing more to do for bike tourists. Music festivals, weekly concerts, food and beverage festivals, and city-sponsored bike events have all increased since mountain biking became a popular tourist sport.

Though some may have tried, mountain bike tourists do not bike all day. Having other events for mountain bike tourists to enjoy post-bike ride or for their non-biking family members was essential to Grand County developing as a summertime tourism market. Ski industry resorts and towns have cashed in on this technique of enhancing sporting experiences through expanding entertainment and retail shopping. The bike towns of Grand County have applied similar tactics.[17]

Cultural Opposition: Resistance to Change

Though Grand County has generally welcomed mountain biking, development of the sport has faced numerous obstacles. Grand County was by no means developed into a mountain bike utopian society. Resistance to change in terms of accepting mountain biking as a new economic driver arose at several levels of Grand County society, as well as across the wide Grand County geographic spectrum. Various organizations, government agencies, and individuals have voiced their concerns about mountain biking. Concerns of mountain biking's impact on the environment, trail usage, traffic, and tradition could be heard from Winter Park to Kremmling.

As outlined in Chapter Three, the United States Forest Service put forth a large effort in converting retired forest service roads into trail systems. They took environmental factors into their trail design and creation. Future expansion projects are handled with the same evaluation process. There have been some areas in Grand County where mountain biking growth was hindered by these regulations.

Hot Sulphur Springs, located between Granby and Kremmling on U.S. Highway 40, lacks a major mountain bike trail system. Environmental concerns of the rare goshawk known to nest in the USFS lands to the south of town have prevented trail expansion beyond the existing forest service roads.[18] Some user created trails were built, but were done so in a non-sustainable manner. These trails tended to be steep, overgrown, or washed out and cannot be found on county trail maps. The user-created routes in Grand County, including the Hot Sulphur trails, added more work for the USFS and added to agency's environmental concerns in regards to mountain bike traffic. Both the USFS environmental policy and rouge trails have slowed building processes in situations such as this. Conflict layered with conflict rarely yields a solution.

The National Park Service is another governmental agency in Grand County that has slowed the expansion of the sport. Rocky Mountain National Park, located north of Grand Lake on U.S. Highway 34, has not allowed mountain bikes on any trails, which is a standard policy for the National Park Service. Preservation has always been the National Park Service's primary approach and mountain biking would have potentially jeopardized the condition of the trails and destroyed wildlife habitat.[19] This policy was challenged in 2012 and mountain bike inclusive trails will be introduced to the parklands on the shore of Grand Lake to connect to USFS lands in 2018. Despite this recent change, mountain biking has not garnered relatively much support in the Grand Lake region.[20]

Traffic and space concerns also showed signs of an anti-mountain biking sentiment. Though there were several trails set up for travel from town to town for non-motorized traffic, congestion on both trails and roads have proven problematic for the communities. In Winter Park and Fraser, accidents between bikers, hikers, runners, and skateboarders have all been noted in recent years, and some have been turned into lawsuits between the competing users.[21] In the local newspaper, motorists criticized bicyclists for riding on the roads, asking them to "get back on the perfectly good bike trails."[22] Crowded trails can be interpreted as a sign of summer tourism growth, but the congestion also creates tension and concerns between mountain bikers, motorists, and pedestrians.

In another example, motorized off-highway users and mountain bikers have clashed over trail use, as many trails were designated for both. Dirt bikes and all-terrain vehicles had concerns of not being allowed on the trails, whereas mountain bikers worried about safety, trail conditions, and noise pollution. These disputes have put the USFS in a position to change the designation of routes.[23] Equine trail users also had a history of not welcoming mountain bike trail users. Several trails in the county were designated routes for horses and bikes, putting them in a similar type of space competition as that of hikers, skateboarders, and pedestrians.

Cultures within a regional sport tourism venue tend to battle for space, as mutually utilized outdoor resources are key to enjoyment. Grand County sport cultures have had to share these resources more than they originally cared to. Similar to the inception of snowboarding on ski resorts, where two distinct cultures were forced to reconcile in order for both sports to thrive, mountain biking in Grand County has continued to compromise with other sport cultures in order to succeed.[24]

Conclusions

Mountain biking has created a cultural shift in Grand County. It would be difficult to deny that the way people live, how they spend their time outdoors, and the way local governments and many businesses operate has changed in the last twenty years to accommodate mountain bikers. Similar to the acceptance of skiing in local culture, mountain biking has brought forth physical change to the towns of Grand County. With such changes came oppositional forces, which confined the growth of the sport to certain areas of the county. The mountain bike industry is still relatively young in comparison to other tourist sports and as the sport continues to grow and evolve, more cultural changes are likely to occur.

7

Ranches, Resorts, and Corporate Mountain Biking

The Current State of Mountain Biking and the Future of the Sport

As experienced in the late 1970s, outside of San Francisco on Mount Tamalpais, mountain biking was raw and underproduced. Bikes were hand-modified, ridden by those who built them, bombing down forest service roads. Getting the bike down the hill in one piece was enough of a challenge, let alone reaching a new course record on the infamous Repack Race. Daily rides exploring the back roads and trails also made up much of mountain biking early days. Riding the never-before traveled and expanding territory gave mountain biking a special place in the cycling world.

Then mountain biking changed. Technology and venues expanded, bringing bikes to all sorts of people in locations across the world. Bikes were created to ride long distances, down steep hills, and jump tens of feet into the air. Riders began to tackle the toughest terrain; rocks, sand, and snow were conquered with diversified bikes.

As the mountain bike industry grew in Grand County, major businesses in the community used it to advance their interests as well. Several major resorts and ranches began offering mountain bike services and integrating mountain bikes into their summertime business plans. Winter Park Resort, Granby Ranch, Devil's Thumb Ranch, and Snow Mountain Ranch all incorporated various types of mountain biking into their summer and winter business models.

Alongside the inception of mountain biking at Grand County resorts, came changes in the sport of biking itself. Though these changes in mountain biking were not by any means solely due to the Grand County biking scene, the businesses within the county do capture the essence of corporate mountain biking, and reflect the extent to which large resort biking areas contribute to the changing sport.

Trestle Bike Park at Winter Park Resort

Winter Park Resort, operated currently by Alterra, has been a major public lands utilizer for decades. The resort has a long history of skiing and snowboarding in the Arapaho National Forest on the southeastern end of Grand County. In the 1930s, after safe travel to Grand County became possible through the Moffat Tunnel and over Berthoud Pass, the Winter Park Ski Area began to develop. The Arlberg Ski Club, which still exists today, had previously cleared trails to ski on. The United States Forest Service and the Civilian Conservation Corps also had trails cleared at the site of the current Winter Park Resort. The various runs were further developed and expanded by the City of Denver, a project driven by George Cranmer. In 1940, with a warming hut and a ski tow, Winter Park opened and soon became a popular destination for Denverites.[1]

During Winter Park Resort's time in the county, they have gone through generations of lift machinery, snow making machines, and mountainside infrastructure. A recent change for Winter Park Resort was the utilization of mountainside amenities for mountain biking. Lifts, business storefronts, and restaurants are now transitioned for summertime use as Winter Park Resort annually morphs from ski town into bike mecca.

Trestle Bike Park, the moniker of the summer bike resort, is a lift-served bike park. The resort utilizes the already in-place ski lift machinery to take mountain bikers, and their bikes, to the top of the mountain. Every other lift chair is removed and replaced with a bike rack of sorts to transport bikes up nearly 2000 feet. Once at the top, a lift attendant unloads the bikes and hands it to the rider, who then continues onto the trail system.

The advantage to this type of operation is that the majority of the riding can be set up downhill with heavier duty bikes and equipment. While downhill riding is still difficult, it takes a different type of fitness than required to pedal up the mountains. Drawing tourists in from lower elevations where oxygen is plentiful, these lifts allow access to parts of the mountain that riders otherwise may not have been able to reach through manpower alone. Downhill runs at Trestle have a wide array of riding, set up in a similar rating system as the resort's ski terrain. Novice riders enjoy riding down green trails, while more advanced riders have a variety of blue and black trails to tackle.[2]

Design for summer and winter lift service share more than just machines; skiing went through this process of ability designation in the early days of resort building. Designers of early ski runs served by lifts attempted to reach terrain of varying difficulty to be used by skiers of varying ability, all while maintaining a sense of independence and serenity.[3]

Each spring, Winter Park Resort opens Trestle Bike Park as soon as they can get trails clear of snow and ready for bikes. A dry snow year may lead to an early bike year. The opposite could occur as well, especially if snow falls late into the spring ski season. The snow controls the fall closure of the bike park, as the resort is committed to opening the skiing and snowboarding operations as soon as scheduling allows. Typically, closing weekend for Trestle Bike Park has fallen in late September, with ski operations starting in mid November.[4]

Winter Park Resort also has hosted several race series at the base of the mountain, as well as at various trailheads around the county. The downhill series has been at the resort, while the Epic Singletrack Series spans the entire summer race season and has been located across the county. The mountain bikers attracted to the race series are generally of fairly affluent socioeconomic status. Sixty-three percent of the races that took the 2012 survey were in a household of $100,000 or more. The socioeconomic well being of this group also allowed them the financial ability to spend more in the county, thus generating more revenue for the local businesses. The racers that came to the Epic Series in 2012 were on average educated family men. Ninety percent held college degrees and 74% were married at the time of the survey.[5] The exit survey suggests that mountain bike racing is not a sport of the poor and has become a source of income for the county through these additional tourists.

Bike Granby Ranch

Northwest of Winter Park Resort is another notable resort, Granby Ranch. This significantly smaller ski resort also makes the summer transition over to biking. The base-to-peak vertical gain is only 1000 feet, which is about half of Winter Park's biking vertical. While Granby Ranch operates in a similar manner as other bike parks in terms of lifts, it lacks some other popular amenities such as a large base area, restaurants, and the multitude of storefronts.[6]

The biking at Bike Granby Ranch is a split of lift-served downhill riding and traditional cross-country riding, and also boasts a large section of lift-served cross-country trails. Lift-served cross-country riding is an uncommon combination, but allows access for several types of bikes and abilities of riders. People intimidated by downhill biking may opt for the slightly less steep grades, minor features, and longer distances. Similar to Trestle Bike Park, the lift saves the rider a lot of climbing and is a major convenience for tourists visiting from lower elevations.

Bike Granby Ranch operates their own rental fleet and pro shop at the base of the resort, but does not have many other commercial attractions to offer outside of fishing and golfing. As to please the more mountain bike purist, they instead have put more recent focus on trail development and event hosting. Jamie Wolter, a director of biking, added several new connector trails, linking the base area of Granby Ranch to the surrounding neighborhoods. Granby Ranch does have a reputation for having a well kept trail system for the past decade, and it is apparent, based on trail map trends, that trail expansion is the current focus.[7]

These neighborhood trails connect homes to trails, which is a plus for the Granby Ranch real estate. Having bike-in, bike-out as a selling point for homes when putting them on the market baits in mountain bike enthusiasts. Whether Granby Ranch is a primary home or a second home, the accessibility to their new trails is marketed as an additional recreation infrastructure.

Events hosted at Granby Ranch are primarily two types of races- downhill events make for short fast time trials and enduro events test riders for several hours across the terrain. These events have grown in number over the past few years and have kept Bike Granby Ranch a sought after destination in both the local Grand County biking scene and the regional Colorado racing scene.

YMCA of the Rockies Snow Mountain Ranch

Over five thousand acres make up a high valley to the south of Red Dirt Hill, a local landmark on U.S. Highway 40 between Fraser and Granby. Tucked under Blue Ridge Mountain lies Snow Mountain Ranch. This branch of the YMCA of the Rockies has developed several facilities across the ranch. The Nordic Center serves as a hub for the winter and summer trail systems. In the winter, groomed trails cover the property for classic, skate skiing, snow shoeing, and most recently fat-tire biking.

Winter biking became a YMCA initiative in 2014, as the fat-tire scene continued to expand. Snow Mountain Ranch began adding trails specifically for these bikes in an effort to keep their ski trails in proper skiing condition. Plans for expansion were started in 2015. That following season, Nordic Director Bill Pierce opened forty kilometers of bike-specific winter trails. These winter biking trails were unique to the YMCA, as the sport was still in the developmental phase. Snow bike trails, such as the ones developed at Snow Mountain Ranch, were slightly widened singletrack, groomed with custom-built packing drags.[8] The increased amount of winter trails significantly raised the total quantity of fat bike trails for both the county and the YMCA. Snow Mountain Ranch previously had ten kilometers of winter riding trails in 2014, making the 2015 expansion a 300% percent increase.[9] In the subsequent years, other entities in the county followed suit, expanding the amount of winter trails in other riding locations across Grand County.

Snow biking aside, the YMCA of the Rockies promotes mountain biking on their grounds during the summer months. Many of the Nordic ski trails double as hiking and biking trails for the non-ski season. Pierce and his trail crew have been overhauling the summer trail system. Inheriting the trail system from previous Nordic Directors, he is dedicated to improving the trails for summer users.

Several of the mountain bike trails built prior to Pierce's arrival needed reworking. Many of the trails were originally built too steep and narrow. This created several problems. For starters, the trails were very difficult to ride, and since the YMCA has traditionally been a family orientated camp, overly difficult trails were inaccessible to most trail users. In addition to this, steep grades and poorly built trails quickly turned to washed out and eroded trail systems. The spring thaw temporarily turned these trails into narrow streambeds. Pierce and his trail building crew have corrected these issues by making new trails with flowing ride lines, and by improving the sustainability of the previously built trails.[10]

Outside of having and maintaining trails, the YMCA also rents bikes at their facility. They have a rental fleet for both summer and winter seasons. These bikes are maintained in a bike shop on campus during the summertime, while operations move to the Nordic Center in the winter months. Managing a fleet of bikes requires clerks and mechanics, creating positions at the YMCA.

Snow Mountain Ranch is also home to many biking events. The Colorado High School Mountain Bike League has hosted large events out of the Nordic Center in years past, as well as Xterra multi-discipline events. Summertime biathlons, combining mountain biking and target shooting, have taken place at the YMCA. More recently, a series of snow biking events started in 2015, as Snow Mountain Ranch aimed to capitalize on the trendy winter sport.[11]

Though not a lift-served biking venue, the YMCA has taken advantage of mountain biking as a tourist sport and has absorbed it into their business model. Providing visitors with a positive mountain biking and snow biking experience is now a major part of summer and winter activities offered at the ranch.

Resorts and Ranches: Changing the Sport

Bike parks, resorts and ranches are abundant in Grand County. These three examples serve as a sample of how these facilities approach of mountain biking activities. To add to the list would be easy as well as redundant. There are other resorts, private facilities, and neighborhoods that host mountain bikers as well. Simply put, biking has become a major aspect of tourism in Grand County, and has in turn become a large part of the county's resorts and ranches. With that being true, it is natural for each facility to embrace the sport. Each business competes to deliver a better product, which in this case is the whole experience of mountain biking. The corporate produced experience is a well-planned and controlled mountain biking experience. This capitalistic competition to improve the experience has spawned new trail systems in several sections of the county on public and private land. These capitalistic endeavors between experience providers have also changed the way the systems are designed.

This concept seems ideal; bikers get better trails and better experiences. On the other hand, the question arises: Do corporate incentives to improve the mountain biking experience align with what is best for the sport? As businesses developed trails with artificial features and large powered lifts, mountain biking has been pulled further from the sport's roots. Mountain biking was founded on low-tech junk bikes riding down forest service roads. The radical contrast from then to now makes mountain biking's transition to professionally designed courses seem hyper-evolutionary.

The scenario for bikers has significantly changed. A first time biker coming to Grand County to test the sport out may have a genuine, backcountry mountain biking experience or they may partake in a more artificial, corporate-molded mountain biking experience. Though people involved in the sport recognize the differences, people new to the sport or uninvolved may not understand those differences. If more and more people are introduced to resort-style biking at the novice level, the sport will continue to be redefined with the corporate influences.

Skiing faced a similar change back in the 1950s and 1960s when several ski areas converted over to ski resorts. Snowmass, Vail Resorts, and Intrawest all extensively expanded operations on both private and approved public lands. As their technology moved forward they were also able to control and shape the experience of skiing. Better lift systems allowed skiing in once hard to reach regions of a mountain. Snow machines made for more consistent snow quality and quantity. Excavating and grooming equipment created skiable terrain for all ages and abilities. Transformations in the way ski resorts operated ultimately changed the experience of skiers and redefined the sport entirely. Being able to create a positive experience for skiers refocused business plans to include expansion, real estate, and base villages. The rugged skiing of the 1940s and small ski towns in the 1960s and 1970s morphed into the resort scene of the 1980s and beyond.[12]

Companies and organizations with mountain biking venues have already begun this process of creating an ideal and consistent biking experience for tourists. Their trail systems and obstacles have started to become a controlled experience. This trend to create flowing trails, many with little-to-no uphill riding, has created a new type of rider as well as a new branch of the industry. As Hal Rothman outlined in *Devil's Bargains*, these changes are typical in tourism in the American West. As tourists change their desires, towns will reflect this by becoming more comforting, convenient, or thrilling places of attraction.[13] While Winter Park mountain biking might not be experiencing *Aspenization*, it is experiencing a similar change to the Disneyesque controlled environments of the modern ski resorts.[14]

Conclusions

Mountain biking is in the midst of a major transformation. Though the young sport was already expanding, major shifts in riding styles have occurred in the past decade. Grand County, Colorado exemplifies these changes at the various mountain bike resorts. Lift service facilities such as Granby Ranch and Trestle Bike Park at Winter Park are both innovative playgrounds with challenging terrain and trails. As these venues alter terrain and trails to provide a more controlled experience, the essence of mountain bike will be redefined as well. Other facilities operating on private and public lands sway the perceived definition of mountain biking, as they aim to please guests with positive experiences. Sports evolve and mountain biking is no exception. Resorts and private biking facilities geared to make money on the sport are happily expediting the evolution.

8

Mountain Bike Capital USA™?

A Sense of Place in the American West

Buoyed by earning the reputation of a premier mountain biking destination, Grand County continued to build on its accomplishments. Expansion projects in both the public and private sectors have put more trails on the map and have brought more people into the county to enjoy them. Changes to trails were apparent across the county. Some were as subtle as a refinished corner or rough patch, while others were new trails and connections, which opened whole new rides. Recently, for example, the USFS better connected two trails, Broken Thumb and Twisted Ankle. These trails created a better connection from the continental divide all the way down to the town of Winter Park, entirely on singletrack and rugged doubletrack, minus a brief stint on a forest service road. Similar connections are being planned by county organizations and make for an ever-changing bike scene.

The rich past of Grand County mountain biking combines with the present push for industrial success. Longtime members of the community, such as Keith Sanders, Meara McQuain and Miles Miller, join forces with passionate newcomers, pushing the mountain bike scene into new levels of growth. Motivation to grow the mountain bike industry comes from both avid local bikers and those seeking financial gain. This combined effort has established a movement with substantial potency.

Mountain Bike Capital USA™ was a bold title to self-proclaim, but Grand County has certainly put forth an earnest effort in becoming just that. The invention of a logo, slogan and use of professional promotion teams create an undeniable capitalistic texture that has engulfed much of the Rockies in outdoor recreation, acting as an additional layer of tourism.[1] As a leader in this movement, the Grand County mountain bike industry stands out as a summertime version Annie Coleman's molded and packaged ski industry.[2] While the boosters of early ski resorts and the promoters of the much newer mountain bike industry are not blood relatives, their industries are akin in their consumables and purchasable experiences.

Grand County as a venue and the individual facilities as sub-venues have become mountain bike friendly and hospitable to visiting outdoors enthusiasts. The massive swaths of state and national public lands are increasingly appreciated in new ways and utilized by different people who otherwise may not see the beauty of Colorado. However, these large lots of public lands available for bikers to explore have raised debates about exploration versus exploitation, and accountability versus accountant's ability. While Grand County continues to develop in a postindustrial economy through the means of tourism, it has ridden the capitalistic reinvention of nature into another season and through another sport. As it does this, Grand County and the rest of the mountain bike industry flirt with the corporatism explored Coleman's *Ski Style* and Rothman's *Devil's Bargain*. Similar to skiing, mountain biking and the culture of the sport is subject to change based on the consumer's desires and corporate ability to deliver experiences.

Not to discredit the many accomplishments of sport and economic growth, but it is doubtful Grand County is the *true* Mountain Bike Capital USA™ and much more likely that the logo is an additional caricature of Grand County's previous identity. Truly, it would be difficult for any community to defend itself as Mountain Bike Capital USA™, due to competing mountain bike scenes and private interests in claiming such a title. Regardless of having this moniker or not, Grand County, Colorado serves as a prime example of a transitioning recreation community, looking to identify with a dominant economic driver.

Grand County's effort to establish an identity relates well to historian Donald Worster writings on the western identity. In *Under Western Skies: Nature and History in the American West*, Worster writes about how the West has had a continually changing identity. Some of the identity is based on the history of the West through the frontier, while the environmental and hydraulic West has acquired its own legacy. Beyond that, he also writes about how the people of the West have created their own self-image. Regionally, it varies by the environment or uniqueness of specific places.[3] Much of Grand County has clearly taken to embracing outdoor recreation as its newest identity. Boosters and promoters pass that identity along to others around the state and country, and while other characteristics and legacies more truly define Grand County's history, its future may very well lie on the trail.

NOTES

Chapter One

[1] Dan Imhoff, *Fat Tire: A Celebration of the Mountain Bike* (San Francisco: Chronicle Books, 1999), 12-20.

[1] Charlie Kelly, *Fat Tire Flyer: Repack and the Birth of Mountain Biking*(Boulder: Velo Press, 2014), 39.

[2] "MTB Paper," e-mail message to author, July 30, 2016.

[3] Meara McQuain and Keith Sanders, interview by author, April 3, 2015.

[4] "Mountain Bike Capital USA | Winter Park, CO," Mountain Bike Capital USA, 2014, Homepage, accessed March 15, 2015, http://mtbcapitalusa.com/.

[5] Robert C. Black, *Island in the Rockies: The Pioneer Era of Grand County, Colorado* (Granby, CO: Published for the Grand County Pioneer Society by the County Printer, 1977), 334-337.

[6] Annie Gilbert. Coleman, *Ski Style: Sport and Culture in the Rockies* (Lawrence, Kan.: University Press of Kansas, 2004), 212-220.

[7] William Philpott, *Vacationland: Tourism and Environment in the Colorado High Country* (Seattle, WA: University of Washington Press, 2013), 300-306.

[8] Hal Rothman, *Devil's Bargains: Tourism in the Twentieth-century American West* (Lawrence, Kan.: University Press of Kansas, 1998), 20-27.

[9] Wallace Stegner, *The American West as Living Space* (Ann Arbor: University of Michigan Press, 1987), 40-44.

[10] Ibid., 70-80.

[11] Gerald D. Nash, *World War II and the West: Reshaping the Economy* (Lincoln: University of Nebraska Press, 1990), 218-226.

[12] "Events Calendar," Play Winter Park, 2014, Events, accessed March 15, 2015, http%3A%2F%2Fplaywinterpark.chambermaster.com%2Fevents%2Fcatgid%2F1

[14] Hal Rothman, *Devil's Bargains,* 16-20.

Chapter Two

[1] Frank J. Berto, *The Birth of Dirt: Origins of Mountain Biking* (San Francisco: Cycling Resources, 1999), 47-50.

[2] Berto, *The Birth of Dirt,* 47-50.

[3] Dan Imhoff, *Fat Tire: A Celebration of the Mountain Bike*, ed. Dan Imhoff (San Francisco: Chronicle Books, 1999), 34-66.

[4] Charlie Kelly, *Fat Tire Flyer: Repack and the Birth of Mountain Biking* (Velo Press, 2014), 99.

[5] Lennard Zinn, "Technical FAQ: Does Wheel Weight Matter? - VeloNews.com," VeloNewscom, June 12, 2012, section goes here, http://velonews.competitor.com/2012/06/bikes-and-tech/technical-faq/technical-faq-does-wheel-weight-matter_223209.

[6] Imhoff, *Fat Tire*, 27.

[7] Imhoff, *Fat Tire*, 21.

[8] Kelly, *Fat Tire Flyer*, 35.

[9] Ibid., 113.

[10] Trek Bicycle Corporation, *Gary Fisher Bikes 2010* (2009), 72.

[11] David Gordon Wilson, Jim Papadopoulos, and Frank Rowland. Whitt,*Bicycling Science*, 3rd ed. (Cambridge, MA: MIT Press, 2004), 358.

[12] Imhoff, *Fat Tire*, 36-47.

[13] Wilson, Papadopoulos, and Rowland. *Bicycling Science*, 440.

[14] Caley Fretz, "UCI to Lift Ban on Disc Brakes in August," VeloNewscom, April 14, 2015, accessed April 20, 2015, http://velonews.competitor.com/2015/04/bikes-and-tech/uci-to-lift-ban-on-disc-brakes-in-august_366590.

[15] "Shootout: Wheel Wars 29 vs 27.5 vs 26," *Mountain Bike Action*, March 2012, accessed March 22, 2015, http://mbaction.com/home-page/home-page-slideshow/shootout-wheel-wars-29-vs-27-5-vs-26.

[16] Matt Wiebe, "Retailers Optimistic but Realistic about Future 650b Sales. (cover Story)," *Bicycle Retailer & Industry News* 21, no. 15 (September 2012): 51-52, accessed March 22, 2015, http://adams.idm.oclc.org/login?url=http://search.ebscohost.com/login.aspx?direct=true&db=bth&AN=79541505&site=ehost-live&scope=site.

[17] Merritt Roe Smith and Leo Marx, *Does Technology Drive History?: The Dilemma of Technological Determinism* (Cambridge, MA: MIT Press, 1994), 2.

[18] Ibid, 19.

[19] Coleman, *Ski Style*, 219-220.

[20] "USA Cycling Rule Book," - USA Cycling, 2015, accessed March 22, 2015, http://www.usacycling.org/news/user/story.php?id=4220.

[21] Specialized, "Specialized Bicycle Components," Specialized Bicycle Components, 2015, accessed April 10, 2015, http://www.specialized.com/us/en/support/archive.

[22] Intrawest, "Trail Map & Stats," Trail Map & Stats, 2014, accessed April 12, 2015, http://trestlebikepark.com/Trail_MapStats.html.

[23] McQuain and Sanders, interview.

[24] "CPI Inflation Calculator," CPI Inflation Calculator, 2017, accessed November 2017, http://data.bls.gov/cgi-bin/cpicalc.pl.

[25] "ATX 27.5 2 - Giant Bicycles," ATX 27.5 2 (2017), 2017, accessed March 6, 2017, https://www.giant-bicycles.com/us/atx-2

[26] Kelly, *Fat Tire Flyer,* 104-115.

[27] Ibid, 128-133.

[28] National Bicycle Dealers Association, "Industry Overview 2015." Accessed June 06, 2016. http://nbda.com/articles/industry-overview-2015-pg34.htm.

[29] Jennifer Walters, "Pedal to the Metal: Mongoose Races to Break From the Pack," *Recreation Marketing,* January 19, 1998, accessed March 4, 2015, EBSCOhost.

[30] Bob Edwards and Ugo Corte. "Commercialization and lifestyle sport: Lessons from 20 years of freestyle BMX in 'Pro-Town, USA'." *Sport in Society* 13, no. 7-8 (2010): 1135-1151.

[31] Lynette Carpiet, "Special Report: Women's Market.," *Bicycle Retailer and Industry News* 23, no. 12 (July 15, 2014), accessed March 4, 2015.

[32] Erinn Morgan, "Niche High-End Mountain Bike Sales Booming Despite Challenges.," *Bicycle Retailer & Industry News* 16, no. 16 (October 2007), accessed March 22, 2015, http://adams.idm.oclc.org/login?url=http://search.ebscohost.com/login.aspx?direct=true&db=bth&AN=26909852&site=ehost-live&scope=site.

[33] Coleman, *Ski Style,* 124-126.

[34] Hal Rothman, *Devil's Bargains,* 19-22.

Chapter Three

[1] Major League Baseball, "Coors Field Information - A-to-Z Guide," Colorado Rockies, accessed April 22, 2016, http://mlb.mlb.com/col/ballpark/information/index.jsp?content=guide.

[2] Philpott *Vacationland*, 21.

[3] Thomas Hinch and James E. S. Higham, *Sport Tourism Development* (Buffalo: Channel View, 2004), 86-87.

[4] Michael W. Childers, *Fire on the Mountain: Growth and Conflict in Colorado Ski Country*, Master's thesis, University of Nevada Las Vegas, 2010, 26-28, accessed July 2016, http://digitalscholarship.unlv.edu/cgi/viewcontent.cgi?article=1252&context=thesesdissertations.

[5] Ibid. 33-36.

[6] Philpott *Vacationland*, 99.

[7] Hinch and Higham, *Sports Tourism Development*, 86-87.

[8] Intrawest, Winter Park Epic Singletrack Race Series Survey 2012, 2012, raw data, Winter Park Resort, Winter Park, CO.

[9] Hinch and Higham, *Sports Tourism Development*, 89-90.

[10] "Colorado.com Colorado Welcomes You," Colorado.com, , accessed April 24, 2016, http://www.colorado.com/travel-information-services/grand-county-colorado-tourism-board.

[11] Hinch and Higham, *Sports Tourism Development*, 90.

[12] Ibid, 90.

[13] Intrawest, "Trail Map & Stats," Trail Map & Stats, 2014, accessed April 12, 2015, http://trestlebikepark.com/Trail_MapStats.html.

[14] Hinch and Higham, *Sports Tourism Development*, 90.

[15] Hal Clifford, *Downhill Slide: Why the Corporate Ski Industry Is Bad for Skiing, Ski Towns, and the Environment* (San Francisco: Sierra Club Books, 2002), 51-53.

[16] Hinch and Higham, *Sports Tourism Development*, 90.

[17] International Mountain Biking Association, "Mountain Bike Trails near Winter Park and Fraiser," MTB Project, , accessed April 24, 2016, http://www.mtbproject.com/directory/8011444/winter-park-and-fraiser.

[18] Hinch and Higham, *Sports Tourism Development*, 90.

[19] Ibid.

[20] Robert C. Black, *Island in the Rockies: The Pioneer Era of Grand County, Colorado* (Granby, CO: Published for the Grand County Pioneer Society by the County Printer, 1977), 336.

[21] Jim Wier, "More Buildings, More Lifts, More Chairs, More People. 1970-1990," *Grand County Historical Association* 9, no. 1 (December 1989): 85.

[22] McQuain and Sanders, interview.

[23] Coleman, *Ski Style*, 153.

[24] Jim Wier, "In the Beginning," *Grand County Historical Association* 9 (December 1989): 4-5.

[25] McQuain and Sanders, Interview.

[26] "History," - COPMOBA, 2016, accessed July 31, 2016, http://www.copmoba.org/history.

[27] "History - Crested Butte Bike Week," Crested Butte Bike Week, 2015, , accessed July 31, 2016, http://cbbikeweek.com/history/.

[28] Ed Zink, "Iron Horse History," Official Tourism Site of Durango, Colorado, , accessed July 29, 2016, http://www.durango.org/press-room/fact-sheets/iron-horse-history.

[29] Hinch and Higham, *Sports Tourism Development*, 163-165.

[30] McQuain and Sanders, Interview.

[31] Penny Hamilton, *Granby, Then and Now: A Quick History* (Granby, CO: Greater Granby Area Chamber of Commerce, 2005), 68-69.

[32] Scott Willoughby, "Winter Park Gears up for Summer with Trestle Bike Park," - The Denver Post, May 20, 2008, accessed April 15, 2015, http://www.denverpost.com/extremes/ci_9316069.

[33] Jason Blevins, "Winter Park Trestle Bike Park Booming with Colorado Freeride Festival," - The Denver Post, August 01, 2013, accessed April 15, 2015, http://www.denverpost.com/ci_23771528/winter-park-trestle-bike-park-booming-colorado-freeride.

Chapter Four

[1] United States Census Bureau, "American FactFinder - Community Facts," American FactFinder - Community Facts, , accessed April 24, 2016, http://factfinder.census.gov/faces/nav/jsf/pages/community_facts.xhtml#.

[2] United States Department of Agriculture, "Sulphur Ranger District," United States Department of Agriculture Forest Service, accessed April 10, 2015, http://www.fs.usda.gov/wps/portal/fsinternet

[3] Miles Miller, interview by author, March 23, 2015.

[4] Miller, interview.

[5] Ibid.

[6] Ibid.

[7] Miller, interview.

[8] Ibid.

[9] Miller, interview.

[10] Ibid.

[11] Miller, interview.

[12] Colorado Parks & Wildlife, *2011-2012 Colorado Off-Highway Vehicle Program Grant Awards* (Littleton, CO: State Trails Program, 2012), 1.

[13] Miller, interview.

[14] Grand County, "Mountain Pine Beetle," Grand County Colorado, 2014, accessed April 10, 2015, http://co.grand.co.us/134/Mountain-Pine-Beetle.

[15] Miller, interview.

[16] Miller, interview.

[17] Ibid.

[18] Miller, interview.

[19] Ibid.

[20] Miller, interview.

[21] United States of America, United States Department of Agriculture Forest Service, Pacific Southwest Research Station, *Mountain Biking: Issues for UDSA Forest Service Managers*, by Deborah Chavez (Albany, CA, 1996), 7-8.

[22] Miller, interview.

[23] McQuain and Sanders, interview.

[24] "Mountain Biking," US Forest Service, accessed April 24, 2016, http://www.fs.fed.us/visit/know-before-you-go/mountain-biking.

[25] Miller, interview.

[26] Keith Sanders, "Fraser Valley Winter Fat Bike Options Expanding Fast," *The Sky-Hi News*, January 15, 2015, section goes here, accessed April 10, 2015, http://www.skyhidailynews.com/news/14650058-113/fraser-valley-winter-fat-bike-options-expanding-fast.

[27] Miller, interview.

Chapter Five

[1] "About," Headwaters Trails Alliance, 2011, accessed May 08, 2015, http://headwaterstrails.org/about/.

[2] Bob Colon, "Resorts Cashing In On Biking Craze," NewsOK.com, July 31, 1988, accessed May 23, 2015, http://newsok.com/resorts-cashing-in-on-biking-craze/article/2234143.

[3] McQuain and Sanders, interview.

[4] Frank J. Berto, *The Birth of Dirt: Origins of Mountain Biking* (San Francisco: Cycling Resources, 1999), 56-57.

[5] "It's Fat Season Again," *Snow Country*, June/July 1990, 22.

[6] "Mountains For Biking," *Snow Country*, June 1989, 27.

[7] "Biking In Ski Country," *Ski*, April 1989, 39.

[8] Bob Colon, "Resorts Cashing In On Biking Craze," NewsOK.com, July 31, 1988, accessed May 23, 2015, http://newsok.com/resorts-cashing-in-on-biking-craze/article/2234143.

[9] McQuain and Sanders, interview.

[10] Ibid.

[11] McQuain and Sanders, interview

[12] Intrawest, "Race Routes & Descriptions," EpicSingleTrack.com -, 2015, section goes here, accessed June 08, 2015, http://www.epicsingletrack.com/routes.html.

[13] McQuain and Sanders, interview.

[14] Philpott *Vacationland,* 19-20.

[15] Maura McKnight, *Headwaters Trails Alliance 2012 Annual Report*, report (Fraser, Colorado, 2013), 2-3.

[16] McQuain and Sanders, interview.

[17] Hal Clifford, *Downhill Slide,* 6-17.

[18] John Monkouski, *BLM Kremmling Field Office OHV Grant Application*, December 2, 2013, Application for road and trail funding for BLM lands near Kremmling Colorado., Kremmling.

[19] BLM, "BLM Colorado | Kremmling Field Office | Mountain Biking, March 19, 2012, accessed June 11, 2015, http://www.blm.gov/co/st/en/fo/kfo/recreation_opportuniti es/mountain_biking.html.

[20] "Trail and Road Maps," Kremmlingchamber.com, 2015, accessed June 22, 2015, http%3A%2F%2Fwww.kremmlingchamber.com%2Fmaps.ht ml.

[21] City of Winter Park, "Finance Department," Finance Department, 2015, accessed June 11, 2015, https://www.colorado.gov/pacific/winterpark/finance-department-2.

[22] McQuain and Sanders, interview.

[23] Hank Shell, "Citizens, Organizers Discuss Grand County Master Trails Plan | SkyHiDailyNews.com," The Sky-Hi News, April 28, 2015, section goes here, accessed June 22, 2015, http://www.skyhidailynews.com/news/16102673-113/citizens-organizers-discuss-grand-county-master-trails-plan.

[24] BLM, *Bureau of Land Management North Fruita Desert Management Plan*, publication, November (2004).

[25] Keith Sanders, "Planning for a Crucial Economic Driver," *Sky-Hi News*(Granby, Colorado), April 17, 2015.

[26] Ibid.

[27] Bil Wengert, *Monthly Sales Tax Report,* report, June 2015, accessed July 05, 2015, https://www.colorado.gov/pacific/winterpark/finance-department-2.

[28] McQuain and Sanders, interview.

[29] BLM, "Kokopelli Trail," Kokopelli Trail, November 6, 2014, accessed July 14, 2015, http://www.blm.gov/ut/st/en/fo/moab/recreation/mountai n_bike_trails/kokopelli_s_trail.html.

Chapter Six

[1] Robert C. Black, *Island in the Rockies: The Pioneer Era of Grand County, Colorado* (Granby, CO: Published for the Grand County Pioneer Society by the County Printer, 1977), 385-387.

[2] Wengert, *Monthly Sales Tax Report,* report, June 2015.

[3] Jim Wier, "The Beginning of Skiing in Grand County," *Grand County Historical Association* 6, no. 1 (March 1988): 9-12.

[4] John Cavanagh, interview by author, May 04, 2015.

[5] Maggie Keller, interview by author, May 06, 2015.

[6] Andy Straus. "Andy Straus on Et Wah." Interview by author. April 17, 2016.

[7] Philpott *Vacationland*, 6-7.

[8] Thomas Hinch and James Higham, *Aspects of Tourism: Sport Tourism Development*, 13th ed. (Buffalo: Channel View, 2004), 108-109.

[9] McQuain and Sanders, interview.

[10] Jeff McCoy, interview by author, May 5, 2015

[11] Keller, interview.

[12] McQuain and Sanders, interview.

[13] Ibid.

[14] McQuain and Sanders, interview.

[15] Ibid.

[16] Debbie Muenster, interview by author, April 02, 2015.

[17] Hal Clifford, *Downhill Slide,* 111.

[18] VJ Valente, interview by author, July 7, 2015.

[19] United States. National Park Service, "Bicycling," National Parks Service, July 01, 2015, accessed July 05, 2015, http://www.nps.gov/romo/planyourvisit/biking.htm.

[20] Associated Press, "Mountain Biking Closer in Rocky Mountain National Park," - The Denver Post, March 28, 2015, accessed July 05, 2015, http://www.denverpost.com/news/ci_27805192/mountain-biking-closer-rocky-mountain-national-park.

[21] Hank Shell, "Felony Charge Filed in Winter Park Skateboard Collision | SkyHiDailyNews.com," The Sky-Hi News, July 30, 2015, section goes here, accessed August 5, 2015, http://www.skyhidailynews.com/news/crime/17485094-113/felony-charge-filed-in-winter-park-skateboard-collision.

[22] Dan Smither, "Letter: Bicyclists Should Use Trails When Available | SkyHiDailyNews.com," The Sky-Hi News, June 18, 2015, accessed July 7, 2015, http://www.skyhidailynews.com/news/16835627-113/letter-bicyclists-should-use-trails-when-available.

[23] Miles Miller, interview by author, March 23, 2015.

[24] Hinch and Higham, *Aspects of Tourism: Sport Tourism Development*, 108-109.

Chapter Seven

[1] Philpott *Vacationland*, 16-18.

[2] Winter Park Resort, "Trail Map," Trail Map, , accessed May 14, 2016, http://trestlebikepark.com/trail_mapstats.html.

[3] Coleman, *Ski Style*, 126-133.

[4] Kyle Wagner, "Trestle Bike Park, Winter Park," The Denver Post, July 07, 2011, , accessed April 14, 2016, http://www.denverpost.com/2011/07/07/trestle-bike-park-winter-park/.

[5] Ibid.

[6] Granby Ranch, "Bike Granby Ranch, Trestle Named among Best in Colorado," Granby Ranch, April 21, 2015, accessed September 03, 2015, http://www.granbyranch.com/press-center/in-the-news/bike-granby-ranch,-trestle-named-among-best-in-colorado.html.

[7] Jamie Wolter, interview by author, September 10, 2015.

[8] Bill Pierson, interview by author, September 15, 2015.

[9] YMCA of the Rockies, "Fat Bike Rental," Snowmountainranch.org, 2014, accessed August 10, 2015, http://snowmountainranch.org/activities/fattirebike/.

[10] Pierson, interview by author.

[11] "Snow Mountain Ranch Fat Bike Races Series – White Out Sprint (Race #1)," Snow Mountain Ranch, accessed April 16, 2016, http://snowmountainranch.org/event/snow-mountain-ranch-fat-bike-races-series-race-1/.

[12] Hal Clifford, *Downhill Slide*, 36-62.

[13] Hal Rothman, *Devil's Bargains*, 338-344.

[14] Hal Clifford, *Downhill Slide*, 128.

Conclusion

[1] Philpott *Vacationland*, 302.

[2] Coleman, *Ski Style*, 217.

[3] Donald Worster, *Under Western Skies: Nature and History in the American West* (New York: Oxford University Press, 1992), 225-237.

BIBLIOGRAPHY
PRIMARY

"ATX 27.5 2 - Giant Bicycles." ATX 27.5 2 (2017). 2017. Accessed March 6, 2017. https://www.giant-bicycles.com/us/atx-2

"Biking In Ski Country." *Ski*, April 1989, 33-42.

Blevins, Jason. "Winter Park Trestle Bike Park Booming with Colorado Freeride Festival." - The Denver Post. August 01, 2013. Accessed April 15, 2015. http://www.denverpost.com/ci_23771528/winter-park-trestle-bike-park-booming-colorado-freeride.

Bureau of Land Management. "BLM Colorado | Kremmling Field Office | Mountain Biking." BLM Colorado | Kremmling Field Office | Mountain Biking. March 19, 2012. Accessed June 11, 2015. http://www.blm.gov/co/st/en/fo/kfo/recreation_opportunities/mountain_biking.html.

Bureau of Land Management. *Bureau of Land Management North Fruita Desert Management Plan*. Publication. November. 2004.

Bureau of Land Management. "Kokopelli Trail." Kokopelli Trail. November 6, 2014. Accessed July 14, 2015. http://www.blm.gov/ut/st/en/fo/moab/recreation/mountain_bike_trails/kokopelli_s_trail.html.

Cavanagh, John. Interview by author. May 04, 2015.

City of Winter Park. "Finance Department." Finance Department. 2015. Accessed June 11, 2015. https://www.colorado.gov/pacific/winterpark/finance-department-2.

Colorado Parks & Wildlife. *2011-2012 Colorado Off-Highway Vehicle Program Grant Awards.* Littleton, CO: State Trails Program, 2012.

Intrawest. "Race Routes & Descriptions." EpicSingleTrack.com -. 2015. Accessed June 08, 2015. http://www.epicsingletrack.com/routes.html.

Intrawest. Winter Park Epic Singletrack Race Series Survey 2012. 2012. Raw data. Winter Park Resort, Winter Park, CO.

Intrawest. "Trail Map & Stats." Trail Map & Stats. 2014. Accessed April 12, 2015. http://trestlebikepark.com/Trail_MapStats.html.

"CPI Inflation Calculator." CPI Inflation Calculator. 2015. Accessed March 2015. http://data.bls.gov/cgi-bin/cpicalc.pl.
Used a value of 1300 and 1980 for a year and converted it into 2015 buying power. Calculator is a part of the Bureau of Labor Statistics.

"Events Calendar." Play Winter Park. 2014. Accessed March 15, 2015. http%3A%2F%2Fplaywinterpark.chambermaster.com%2Fevents%2Fcatgid%2F1

"It's Fat Season Again." *Snow Country*, June/July 1990, 22.

Keller, Maggie. Interview by author. May 06, 2015.

McKnight, Maura. *Headwaters Trails Alliance 2012 Annual Report*. Report. Fraser, Colorado, 2013.

McQuain, Meara, and Keith Sanders. Interview by author. April 3, 2015.

Miller, Miles. Interview by author. March 23, 2015.

Monkouski, John. *BLM Kremmling Field Office OHV Grant Application*. December 2, 2013. Application for road and trail funding for BLM lands near Kremmling Colorado., Kremmling.

"Mountain Bike Capital USA | Winter Park, CO." Mountain Bike Capital USA. 2014. Accessed March 15, 2015. http://mtbcapitalusa.com/.

"Mountain Biking." US Forest Service. Accessed April 24, 2016. http://www.fs.fed.us/visit/know-before-you-go/mountain-biking.

"Mountains For Biking." *Snow Country*, June 1989, 27.

"MTB Paper." E-mail message to author. July 30, 2016. Keith Sanders followed up to some additional questions I had for him on the early stages of the mountain bike scene in Grand County.

Muenster, Debbie. Interview by author. April 02, 2015.

Pierson, Bill. Interview by author. September 15, 2015.

Ritchey International. *Ideas Never Sleep.* Grancia-Lugano, Switzerland: Ritchey, 1997.

Shell, Hank. "Felony Charge Filed in Winter Park Skateboard Collision | SkyHiDailyNews.com." The Sky-Hi News. July 30, 2015. Accessed August 5, 2015. http://www.skyhidailynews.com/news/crime/17485 094-113/felony-charge-filed-in-winter-park-skateboard-collision.

Shell, Hank. "Citizens, Organizers Discuss Grand County Master Trails Plan | SkyHiDailyNews.com." The Sky-Hi News. April 28, 2015. Accessed June 22, 2015. http://www.skyhidailynews.com/news/16102673-113/citizens-organizers-discuss-grand-county-master-trails-plan.

Smither, Dan. "Letter: Bicyclists Should Use Trails When Available | SkyHiDailyNews.com." The Sky-Hi News. June 18, 2015. Accessed July 7, 2015. http://www.skyhidailynews.com/news/16835627-113/letter-bicyclists-should-use-trails-when-available.

"Snow Mountain Ranch Fat Bike Races Series – White Out Sprint (Race #1)." Snow Mountain Ranch. Accessed April 16, 2016. http://snowmountainranch.org/event/snow-mountain-ranch-fat-bike-races-series-race-1/.

Specialized. "Specialized Bicycle Components." Specialized Bicycle Components. 2015. Accessed April 10, 2015. http://www.specialized.com/us/en/support/archive.

Straus, Andy. "Andy Straus on Et Wah." Interview by author. April 17, 2016.

Trek Bicycle Corporation. *Gary Fisher Bikes 2010*. 2009.

"Trail and Road Maps." Kremmlingchamber.com. 2015. Accessed June 22, 2015. http%3A%2F%2Fwww.kremmlingchamber.com%2Fm aps.html.

United States Census Bureau. "American FactFinder - Community Facts." American FactFinder - Community Facts. Accessed April 24, 2016. http://factfinder.census.gov/faces/nav/jsf/pages/co mmunity_facts.xhtml#.

United States Department of Agriculture. "Sulphur Ranger District." United States Department of Agriculture Forest Service. Accessed April 10, 2015. http://www.fs.usda.gov/wps/portal/fsinternet.

United States of America. United States Department of Agriculture Forest Service. Pacific Southwest Research Station. *Mountain Biking: Issues for UDSA Forest Service Managers*. By Deborah Chavez. Albany, CA, 1996. 1-33.

"USA Cycling Rule Book." - USA Cycling. 2015. Accessed March 22, 2015. http://www.usacycling.org/news/user/story.php?id= 4220.

Valente, VJ. Interview by author. July 7, 2015.

Wagner, Kyle. "Trestle Bike Park, Winter Park." The Denver
    Post. July 07, 2011. Accessed April 14, 2016.
    http://www.denverpost.com/2011/07/07/trestle-
    bike-park-winter-park/.

Walters, Jennifer. "Pedal to the Metal: Mongoose Races to
    Break From the Pack." *Recreation Marketing*, January
    19, 1998. Accessed March 4, 2015. EBSCOhost.

Wengert, Bil. *Monthly Sales Tax Report.* Report. June 2015.
    Accessed July 05, 2015.
    https://www.colorado.gov/pacific/winterpark/financ
    e-department-2.

Willoughby, Scott. "Winter Park Gears up for Summer with
    Trestle Bike Park." - The Denver Post. May 20, 2008.
    Accessed April 15, 2015.
    http://www.denverpost.com/extremes/ci_93160

Winter Park Resort. "Trail Map." Trail Map. Accessed May 14,
    2016. http://trestlebikepark.com/trail_mapstats.html.

Wolter, Jamie. Interview by author. September 10, 2015.

YMCA of the Rockies. "Fat Bike Rental."
    Snowmountainranch.org. 2014. Accessed August 10,
    2015.
    http://snowmountainranch.org/activities/fattirebike/.

YMCA of the Rockies. "Mountain Biking." Snow Mountain
    Ranch. 2015. Accessed September 03, 2015.
    http://snowmountainranch.org/activities/mountain-
    biking/.

SECONDARY

"About." Headwaters Trails Alliance. 2011. Accessed May 08, 2015. http://headwaterstrails.org/about/.

Associated Press. "Mountain Biking Closer in Rocky Mountain National Park." - The Denver Post. March 28, 2015. Accessed July 05, 2015. http://www.denverpost.com/news/ci_27805192/mountain-biking-closer-rocky-mountain-national-park.

Berto, Frank J. *The Birth of Dirt: Origins of Mountain Biking.* San Francisco: Cycling Resources, 1999.

Black, Robert C. *Island in the Rockies: The Pioneer Era of Grand County, Colorado.* Granby, CO: Published for the Grand County Pioneer Society by the County Printer, 1977.

Carpiet, Lynette. "Special Report: Women's Market." *Bicycle Retailer and Industry News* 23, no. 12 (July 15, 2014): 1-18. Accessed March 4, 2015.

Childers, Michael W. *Fire on the Mountain: Growth and Conflict in Colorado Ski Country.* Master's thesis, University of Nevada Las Vegas, 2010. 1-237. Accessed July 2016. http://digitalscholarship.unlv.edu/cgi/viewcontent.cgi?article=1252&context=thesesdissertations.

Clifford, Hal. *Downhill Slide: Why the Corporate Ski Industry Is Bad for Skiing, Ski Towns, and the Environment.* San Francisco: Sierra Club Books, 2002.

Coleman, Annie Gilbert. *Ski Style: Sport and Culture in the Rockies*. Lawrence, Kan.: University Press of Kansas, 2004.

Colon, Bob. "Resorts Cashing In On Biking Craze." NewsOK.com. July 31, 1988. Accessed May 23, 2015. http://newsok.com/resorts-cashing-in-on-biking-craze/article/2234143.

"Colorado.com Colorado Welcomes You." Colorado.com. Accessed April 24, 2016. http://www.colorado.com/travel-information-services/grand-county-colorado-tourism-board.

Dunning, Ed. *Mountain Bike Rentals, Sales, and Repairs: The Basics for Starting a Bike Program*. Report. Walton Beach: Bureau of Naval Personnel, 1998. Accessed March 4, 2015. EBSCOhost.

Edwards, Bob, and Ugo Corte. "Commercialization and lifestyle sport: Lessons from 20 years of freestyle BMX in 'Pro-Town, USA'." *Sport in Society* 13, no. 7-8 (2010): 1135-1151.

Fretz, Caley. "UCI to Lift Ban on Disc Brakes in August." VeloNewscom. April 14, 2015. Accessed April 20, 2015. http://velonews.competitor.com/2015/04/bikes-and-tech/uci-to-lift-ban-on-disc-brakes-in-august_366590.

Granby Ranch. "Bike Granby Ranch, Trestle Named among Best in Colorado." Granby Ranch. April 21, 2015. Accessed September 03, 2015. http://www.granbyranch.com/press-center/in-the-news/bike-granby-ranch,-trestle-named-among-best-in-colorado.html.

Granby Ranch. "Downhill and Cross-Country Mountain Biking." Colorado Mountain Biking – Bike Activities –. September 2015. Accessed October 01, 2015. http://www.granbyranch.com/bike-granby-ranch/bike.html.

Grand County. "Mountain Pine Beetle." Grand County Colorado. 2014. Accessed April   10, 2015. http://co.grand.co.us/134/Mountain-Pine-Beetle.

Hamilton, Penny. *Granby, Then and Now: A Quick History.* Granby, CO: Greater Granby Area Chamber of Commerce, 2005.

Hinch, Thomas, and James Higham. *Aspects of Tourism: Sport Tourism Development.* 13th ed. Buffalo: Channel View, 2004.

"History - Crested Butte Bike Week." Crested Butte Bike Week. 2015. Accessed July 31, 2016. http://cbbikeweek.com/history/. "History." - COPMOBA. 2016. Accessed July 31, 2016. http://www.copmoba.org/history.

"History." Headwaters Trails Alliance. 2011. Accessed May 08, 2015. http://headwaterstrails.org/about/history/.

Industry Overview 2015. - National Bicycle Dealers
    Association. Accessed June 06, 2016.
    http://nbda.com/articles/industry-overview-2015-
    pg34.htm.

International Mountain Biking Association. "Mountain Bike
    Trails near Winter Park and Fraiser." MTB Project.
    Accessed April 24, 2016.
    http://www.mtbproject.com/directory/8011444/wint
    er-park-and-fraiser.

Imhoff, Dan, Dan Koeppel, Joe Breeze, Mark Reidy, and Jenny
    Fenster. *Fat Tire: A Celebration of the Mountain Bike.*
    Edited by Dan Imhoff. San Francisco: Chronicle Books,
    1999.

Kelly, Charlie. *Fat Tire Flyer: Repack and the Birth of Mountain
    Biking.* Velo Press, 2014.

Major League Baseball. "Coors Field Information - A-to-Z
    Guide." Colorado Rockies. Accessed April 22, 2016.
    http://mlb.mlb.com/col/ballpark/information/index.j
    sp?content=guide.

Morgan, Erinn. "Niche High-End Mountain Bike Sales Booming
    Despite Challenges." *Bicycle Retailer & Industry News*
    16, no. 16 (October 2007): 42-43. Accessed March 22,
    2015.
    http://adams.idm.oclc.org/login?url=http://search.ebs
    cohost.com/login.aspx?direct=true&db=bth&AN=2690
    9852&site=ehost-live&scope=site.

Nash, Gerald D. *World War II and the West: Reshaping the Economy*. Lincoln: University of Nebraska Press, 1990.

Norman, Jason. "Full-Suspsension Mountain Bikes, Hybrids Take Flight at IBDs." *Bicycle Retailer and Industry News* 17, no. 5 (April 2008): 37-38. Accessed March 4, 2015.

Philpott, William. *Vacationland: Tourism and Environment in the Colorado High Country*. Seattle, WA: University of Washington Press, 2013.

"Recent Data Show Mountain Bike Sales Climbing." *IMBA Trail News* 26, no. 3 (2013): 4. Accessed March 22, 2015. http://adams.idm.oclc.org/login?url=http://search.ebs cohost.com/login.aspx?direct=true&db=s3h&AN=9193 2105&site=ehost-live&scope=site.

Rothman, Hal. *Devil's Bargains: Tourism in the Twentieth-century American West*. Lawrence, Kan.: University Press of Kansas, 1998.

Sanders, Keith. "Fraser Valley Winter Fat Bike Options Expanding Fast." *The Sky-Hi News*, January 15, 2015. Accessed April 10, 2015. http://www.skyhidailynews.com/news/14650058-113/fraser-valley-winter-   fat-bike-options-expanding-fast.

Sanders, Keith. "Planning for a Crucial Economic Driver." *Sky-Hi News* (Granby, Colorado), April 17, 2015.

"Shootout: Wheel Wars 29 vs 27.5 vs 26." *Mountain Bike Action*, March 2012. Accessed March 22, 2015. http://mbaction.com/home-page/home-page-slideshow/shootout-wheel-wars-29-vs-27-5-vs-26.

Stegner, Wallace. *The American West as Living Space*. Ann Arbor: University of Michigan Press, 1987.

Vidergar, Cyril. "Grand County Living Magazine - Keith Sanders and the Emergence of the Fraser Valley Mountain Bike Scene." Grand County Living Magazine - Keith Sanders and the Emergence of the Fraser Valley Mountain Bike Scene. Summer 2010. Accessed May 10, 2015. http://grandcountyliving.com/articles2010/summer/features10_MtbSanders.html

United States. National Park Service. "Bicycling." National Parks Service. July 01, 2015. Accessed July 05, 2015. http://www.nps.gov/romo/planyourvisit/biking.htm.

Wiebe, Matt. "Retailers Optimistic but Realistic about Future 650b Sales. (cover Story)." *Bicycle Retailer & Industry News* 21, no. 15 (September 2012): 1-50. Accessed March 22, 2015. http://adams.idm.oclc.org/login?url=http://search.ebscohost.com/login.aspx?direct=true&db=bth&AN=79541505&site=ehost-live&scope=site.

Wier, Jim. "In the Beginning." *Grand County Historical Association* 9 (December 1989): 3-24.

Wier, Jim. "More Buildings, More Lifts, More Chairs, More People. 1970-1990." *Grand County Historical Association* 9, no. 1 (December 1989): 73-88.

Wier, Jim. "The Beginning of Skiing in Grand County." *Grand County Historical Association* 6, no. 1 (March 1988): 9-12.

Wilson, David Gordon, Jim Papadopoulos, and Frank Rowland. Whitt. *Bicycling Science*. 3rd ed. Cambridge, MA: MIT Press, 2004.

Worster, Donald. *Under Western Skies: Nature and History in the American West*. New York: Oxford University Press, 1992.

Zink, Ed. "Iron Horse History." Official Tourism Site of Durango, Colorado. Accessed July 29, 2016. http://www.durango.org/press-room/fact-sheets/iron-horse-history.

Zinn, Lennard. "Technical FAQ: Does Wheel Weight Matter? - VeloNews.com." VeloNewscom. June 12, 2012. http://velonews.competitor.com/2012/06/bikes-and-tech/technical-faq/technical-faq-does-wheel-weight-matter_223209.

Made in the USA
San Bernardino, CA
16 December 2019